Truth or
Counterfeits

JUDY PARROTT
Heavens Hands Publications©

Introduction

If we know the genuine article, the Bible, like the bank clerks who study real money to recognize counterfeits, we will not be deceived. The beliefs of every religion oppose the truth of Christianity, especially who Jesus Christ really is. This book reveals some belief systems to recognize and avoid.

We are entering an era in history that is unique. The return of Christ is on the horizon. Most of the prophecies have now been fulfilled. Spiritual warfare has always existed, but Satan is coming, with great wrath, to the end of his time. "Many will fall away in the last days." We are advised to be wise as a serpent and gentle as a lamb. One thing to remember is *we can't use God*. We can only agree with Him. He is the Boss.

Beth has quite a story. "I relaxed my pen over the paper, thinking about what food I needed at the grocery store. Then the pen started writing automatically, "Call me." I was shocked! I dropped it as if it was on fire! I rebuked it, and sent it away in Jesus' name. Then I prayed. Later, I thanked God, because it hit me. The demon no longer had power over me. He needed my invitation to enter my life again. This time, and for eternity, he doesn't have my permission. Jesus set me free, and I am free indeed!" Look for the whole story under "Hands Off my Ouija Board!" It begins on page 104.

Most of us are stunned to learn that we have been exposed to the occult (meaning hidden or secret things) during our lives. When I was a child, my relatives used to entertain themselves by "table tipping", having no idea they were dabbling in the occult! (Old 'parlor game' in which spirits lift a table and tip a side to answer, known to lift people off the floor and do shocking things.)

Nearly every family (and church) in America is affected one way or another by evil spirits of some kind. We can prepare to set the captives free if we understand how simple it is. Jesus left instructions to heal the sick, cast out devils, and preach the gospel until He returns. Mark 16:16-19 Freedom is wonderful. Why let anyone suffer when we have the authority and the power through Christ to change lives?

Many will fall away in the last days. 2 Timothy 3:1 says, "This know also that in the last days perilous times shall come." I John 5:19 says, "We know that we are of God, and the whole world lies *under the sway of* the wicked one." NKJV

This book prepares God's children for the last days. We are confronted with the New Age, Humanism, Satanism and Postmodernism. Only 4% American Christians have a Biblical worldview, 8% believe all points of the Apostle's Creed, and 91% bought into the lies about Christianity. (GeoBarna.com) This is called the Post-Christian Era. Are we headed for extinction as Christians? Even Jesus said, "Will I find faith on the earth when I return?"

Can people involved in the occult be helped? The occult is an extremely dangerous area in which to operate, so you must be careful.

Talk to them to find what needs and problems they are facing. Be sure not to be angry with anyone who is involved. God is Love. Most have been searching for the truth. Share your faith in Jesus Christ, and the fact He is the only answer to their difficulties. Point out the authority and victory of Christ over the occult world and His power over Satan. He offers victory over all who will believe in Him and trust Him as their Lord and Savior. Be sure and trust the Holy Spirit as your guide to share the Good News of deliverance.

We offer to the world, Jesus Christ crucified and risen, without compromise, apology, or argument, but with gentleness and loving kindness. Charles Spurgeon said, "The gospel is like a caged lion. It does not need to be defended; it just needs to be let out of its cage."

Everyone has questions about the dark side. You are about to read some shocking information about its existence and how to prevent it or overcome it in your own life. Yes, even you are exposed to this invisible realm every day of your life. Be informed and you will conquer every one of these invisible powers and principalities!

Table of Contents

A Course in Miracles

Oprah has offered a training course to the world over the Internet believing it is beneficial for reinterpreting Christian principles. "A Course in Miracles" sounds delightful. Who does not enjoy a miracle? It was very generous of her to do this. Sadly, it is not benign as it appears to be. It began in 1965. An atheist Jewish psychologist college teacher wrote three books. She learned how to 'channel' and received the information during automatic writing and claimed it came from Jesus Christ. This is "another Jesus" the Bible warns us about.

Channeling is a forbidden practice. (Deut. 18:9-12). Spirits not from God do tricks to deceive, eventually control and destroy God's creation- man. (2 Cor. 4:4).

Someone allows or invites a spirit to possess him or her usually for psychic knowledge or power, healing, or to use the person's voice to speak to give spiritual teachings or advice. Various forms of spirit communication exist, such as automatic writing, narrated visions, and inner voice dictation. Genesis 3:1 (cf. 2 Corinthians 11:5, 13-16).

Channeling works through meditation, relaxation, visualization, hypnosis, altered states of consciousness, and other methods. Channelers claim the spirits enter, possess, and control them, promising wisdom from spirits, who have "passed on" and are "highly evolved". These counterfeits of the Holy Spirit are under Satan's orders to possess men. They have a vested interest in being friendly, but lead to bondage, mental disorders, physical danger, and much more. Satan is not a nice boss.

Note: The New Age Movement as a whole is largely undergirded by channeled revelations and activities (cf., our *The Facts on Spirit Guides*, Harvest House, 1988).

Broken Chains

My name is Lana, a Jewish girl from Long Island, New York. I have a twin brother named Louie. We grew up with a gay, alcoholic father, who physically and emotionally battered us at every opportunity. As a result of such a terribly dysfunctional childhood, I got involved with men, drugs, and rock n' roll to kill the pain. I became a cocaine addict, and had sex with lots of men.

The pain increased, and I could never figure out why nothing ever satisfied me. I had a continual lust for more. In March 1991 my father died of cancer, and had never accepted the Lord Jesus Christ. My dad had made monetary provisions for my brother and me, and I decided to open up my own business because my life was going nowhere fast, and nothing I had done up until that point was meaningful.

I opened a music store thinking that owning a business would satisfy me, and make my life worth living. One of my customers named Danielle told me she was a hairdresser, and that she loved the color of my hair (it was red at the time) so I decided to give her a shot at it. (She didn't tell me she was a charismatic Christian.) As she did my hair she started telling me about the Lord Jesus, and we became good friends.

She bought me my first Bible, and invited me to Bible studies at her house, and even took me to a prayer meeting where healings occurred. I told my friend Theresa about this and she started joining the Bible studies with Danielle and me. Theresa's cousins belonged to a Pentecostal church on Long Island, and one day she asked me to come with her.

I went with her one Sunday morning and as the service was going on people were dancing, jumping around, speaking in other languages, raising their hands, and some were crying. I did not understand what all this meant, and I thought everyone was crazy. I had to leave the church and smoke a cigarette to calm myself down. I went back in, and something cut me in the heart. I wanted to cry but I couldn't. Some lady ministered to me outside while I was smoking, gave me her phone number and a Bible to read.

A few days later I called her and told her I was reading the Bible she gave me, though I could hardly understand it. She led me to pray the 'sinner's prayer' and I asked Jesus to come into my heart. I did not realized it meant the same Spirit that raised Jesus Christ from the dead now lived inside of me! Seeds were being planted that would begin to grow, but I was not yet aware of that.

Time went on and I became depressed to the point of suicide. My business did not bring me the peace I had hoped for. My family life grew worse and worse, and I was living with my boyfriend/business partner at that time, who did not want me going to Bible studies. A few venereal diseases, two abortions, my father dying, getting rid of my business and losing my investment began to take a toll on my ability to cope with life. I moved from one friend's house to another, boyfriend to boyfriend, groping in the dark, looking to possessions and people to remove the pain. I needed something to make me whole!

Reaching one last time, I called my twin in California and asked him if I could come out there. Maybe getting out of New York would help me.

Before I left, my brother told me about a woman he had met in a trendy bar in L.A. In a psychic reading, she had told him about his past, and future (so he thought), and even described me perfectly, down to the color car I drive. She was a witch, and got her information from the devil. She told him amazing things nobody could have known.

August 17, 1993, I left for California. Louie had become a very successful stockbroker, just as Audrey had predicted. I was anxious to meet her. When we met, she told me she works for the Beverly Hills Police Department, solving murders and crimes. She said that Jesus came to her in her dreams right before she would have to solve a crime. I then asked her about Jesus, because I learned bits and pieces in the past about the Lord. She told me she does not believe that he is the Son of God, and then she said, "And you don't either. Right?"

I was impressed at the time but the precious Holy Spirit revealed to me later that demons observe us. That is how they know the past. They do not know the future, but they try to deceive us when we go to fortunetellers or read 'horrorscopes'. They tell us stuff they want to do to us, and by being deceived and believing it; we then bring it to pass.

The novelty of being in trendy Los Angeles wore off after many attempts to find happiness (in sex and drugs) I started to get very depressed, actually suicidal, and constantly thought of ways to kill myself. I was hanging around with Audrey almost on a daily basis. She would tell me about "Karma", spirit guides, and other things that are now repulsive to me as a Christian. Audrey introduced me to a guy named Matthew, who became my boyfriend in California.

His cousin and girlfriend were heavily involved in the "New Age" movement, and meditated and changed with crystals, studied humanism, and were into angels and other things. My cousin Andy, who lives with my brother, is into these things as well; incense, candles, crystals, and this really weird statue thing he would meditate with or to; I have no idea.

I was also having problems because of the stress I had to deal with. My life was out of control. I had a stomach ulcer, and used laxatives, teas, and other herbs from the New Age health food store. I contacted someone in the phone book who gave colonics (high powered enemas) so I could get some relief, not knowing he was a witch doctor/warlock who practiced some other kind of "New Age" ritual nonsense.

I now understand why I was so depressed. I had all these demons around me, oppressing me, and wanting me to kill myself so that I would go to hell. Satan, you lost again; you are a liar!!

While I was in California, my mom called Danielle in New York, and another Christian friend in Florida who prayed for our relationship to be healed, and January 17, 1993, an earthquake rocked California. Two days after I left. Before I left California, I gave my brother Louie the Bible Danielle bought me, and a beautiful porcelain cross, and even taught my brother how to look up scriptures.

My mom told me God answered her prayer, and that God made the earthquake for her so I would come to Georgia and have a chance at restoring our relationship.

I came to live in Georgia with my mom after the earthquake. Soon after I arrived in Georgia, I needed a haircut, so mom introduced me to Wynn, her hairdresser, who used to attend Landmark Church. He told me how the Lord healed him of AIDS, and that he wanted to minister to AIDS patients.

Mom and I attended a couple prayer meetings, and at one, a lady named June led my mom in a prayer to ask Jesus into her heart. When mom prayed, she said, "OOH, my heart! It just got really hot!!"

At this time I was working for a temporary agency as a secretary, hoping to find permanent employment, and even started working as a cashier at Wal-Mart for extra money at night. A couple I had never met before invited me to the Atlanta Church of Christ. I did, but it did not work out because it was not a spirit-filled church. The scripture reads in Galatians 3:3: Are ye so foolish? Having begun in the Spirit, are ye now made perfect by the flesh?

I received a call from Audrey (the witch) and she told me she was coming to Atlanta. Coincidence? I don't think so! I told her about my new friends and the church I was attending. She mocked it, because we are both Jewish, and she does not believe Jesus is the Son of God, but does profess Jesus comes to her in her dreams, to help her solve crimes. Pray for Audrey. She came to spend a week with an old boyfriend.

I tried to see her often because I knew she was only there for a week. She came to my mom's house, spent time with my family, and gave a psychic reading to my little brother Joey. She told him something he had already done, another trick of Satan. Then she started teaching them how to meditate. As you can see, Audrey, a practicing witch, had met my entire family in California. Satan was out to deceive my whole family, but God still sits on the throne, and He is the same, yesterday, today and forever.

Shortly after Audrey returned home, things started happening to our relationships in the family. (Gee, I wonder why?) A friend from Landmark prayed a prayer of deliverance and broke all the curses that were on me.

Things went from awesome to terrible in about a month, leading mom to kick me out of the house. I asked Audrey's boyfriend if I could stay there until I found a place.

While there, I found an apartment and got a permanent job at USA TODAY. My car quit as I stopped to get gas in Lawrenceville. I saw a man using the pay phone at the station. As I was cursing out my car, he walked up and asked me if I needed a hand. He learned it was the battery. He was very kind and helped me pick out a battery at K-Mart, and even installed it for me! I was speechless. I could not believe the kindness I was shown. He told me he had to go, and I asked him to sit in my car for a minute while I smoked a cigarette. He then proceeded to give me his testimony.

He told me he had a fatal car accident a few years ago (because he and his friend were drinking and doing drugs) and that he died, had an experience/warning from heaven, and ever since then, he told me he has re-dedicated his life to the Lord. This was an obvious message from the Lord.

I thought about this stuff, and started reading this book I had taken from a friend in New York. It had been with me in the trunk of my car for as long as I can remember…the Holy Bible!

One night I went to bed (alone, just in case you were wondering), and felt something all over me, touching me in a sexual way. I knew that I was not having a nightmare, because I had not even fallen asleep yet. Just as I realized what was happening, this thing covered my mouth and kept me from calling out to Jesus for help. I made a few attempts, and finally I was able to just barely get the words out, "Jesus, Jesus!" I jumped out of bed, grabbed my Bible, and put on TBN. I was lying on my couch, clutching my Bible to my chest for dear life, and laying in a pool of my own sweat. I did not know what to do and couldn't call anyone I knew, because I thought no one would believe me anyway, so why bother?

I stayed on the couch, praying for morning to come. That same night, I heard an audible voice coming from my kitchen, (the doors were locked!) but I was so paralyzed with fear, I blocked it out of my mind. All hell was literally breaking loose in my apartment, and I did not understand why.

Exhausted from the trauma, and very confused, I continued to read the Bible, and watch TBN. Every pastor that came on TBN was ministering to me, and Carlton Pearson, in a sermon, said," If you have never butted heads with the devil at one time or another, there is a good chance that you are walking with him."

That statement shed some light on why this situation had happened to me. I was starting to seek out the truth, and the enemy tried to stop me, but lost again!

I lived in torment for weeks, demons flying over my bed calling my name in the night and waking me, flickering lights bringing fear and sleepless nights, loneliness, days and nights of crying myself to sleep. Several pastors on TBN had stressed how important it was to find a good church and have fellowship with like-minded people, but I just did not even know where to start looking for a church!

Then one day T.D. Jakes was preaching on "The woman with the issue of blood." She said to herself," If I could only touch the hem of His garment, I would be healed." So Pastor Jakes, in closing his sermon, said, "Sometimes we have to minister to ourselves". I remembered that my friend Wynn told me he went to Landmark Church.

I showed up at Landmark on a Wednesday night. Jeanette Kelly introduced me to Anna and Isla. There was an altar call that night, so I went up to the altar crying. With mascara running down my face, I suddenly opened my eyes to see feet; not just any feet, mind you, but feet with freckles and no shoes!

I started to laugh, and said to God, " You're kidding, right?" This guy, Mark, asked me what I wanted to pray for. I told him I just wanted to thank the Lord Jesus because He is awesome. Mark prayed for me and I started attending the church.

Jesus is now the Lord of my life. Louie asked Jesus into his heart, and so did my little brothers. God has healed my ulcer and all the other problems. He has delivered me from nicotine, and I am able to jog over an hour without being short of breath.

The Lord showed me the veil of darkness hovering over those that are not completed Jews. Jesus is not a choice. He is the promised Messiah. He has the words of eternal life. We cannot live without Him.

My Grace Walk
By Ann P.

"Consider it pure joy, my brothers, whenever you face trials of many kinds, because you know that the testing of your faith develops perseverance. Perseverance must finish its work so that you may be mature and complete, not lacking anything."
"If any of you lacks wisdom, he should ask God, who gives generously to all without

finding fault, and it will be given to him."
James 1:2-5

Mom was an alcoholic; Dad was a leader in his profession, but not in the home. Both worked. Dad also went to school, a lot. Dad was a professed Christian; his mother, my precious grandmother, was a practicing Christian. I believe she prayed me into the Kingdom. Mom was agnostic, a feminist who used to say, "If God had intended us to get up with the sun, she would have made it rise later in the day."

My mother was also a practicing "witch". She read palms and tarot cards. Fortunately for me, God protected me from that bondage. Whenever I would ask her to read my palm, she would have an excuse, be it my age or some other reason.

Born in Florida, raised in Augusta, Georgia, I am the youngest of four children. I have one wonderful brother, who has a wife and two kids, and one brother who is probably living in some sort of shelter. I did receive word recently that he is alive, but will not contact any of us. This is after a year and a half of no contact, for the second time since Mom died. My sister is one the kindest most generous, gentle spirited people you will ever meet. She is also a lesbian, bless her heart. Her partner of twenty years committed suicide about two years ago, shortly after they "divorced". Imagine that. It was a major loss for me as well, as her partner was like a big sister to me for twenty years.

My older brothers and sister were into cigarettes and pot, so I followed suit. I started smoking cigarettes when I was twelve, and pot when I was thirteen. I started on pills when I was fifteen. The very first time I tried them, a twenty-nine-year-old friend of my brother's molested me. You would think I would have learned. I then wanted to be high even more to cover the pain. I became quite promiscuous since everyone else was doing it, and my brother's friend had let me know by his actions that I wasn't worth any more than that. At least that is the lie I believed.

By the time I was seventeen I had an abortion. Shortly after that, I moved out because of my mother's verbal abuse. I lived in a cottage behind my sister's house. My oldest brother and sister thought it would be a good idea for me to get involved in transcendental meditation. Not! I went to four out of five classes. Fortunately the last class, the one in which you actually go into the "trance", was cancelled. I tried it anyway, from what I had learned. This is what happened. My soul completely left my body, hovering in total, eerie, darkness. It scared the daylights out of me and scared my soul back into my body. I don't want to go there again.

Six months after I moved into the cottage, my Dad offered to send me to college if I moved back home. So, I moved home, started college, and two weeks later my Dad died of a heart attack.

By the time I was twenty-one, I had an Associate Degree in Mechanical Engineering. I actually moved in with my sister for my last four months of school because of my mother's verbal abuse. I loved my mother, but I couldn't live with her when she was drinking, which was every day.

I took my degree, and moved to Atlanta. I decided school was my discipline, so I went back part time, working full time as a drafter. Going to school kept me from partying, most of the time . . . during the week. I thought I was all set, but I kept having this emotional pain that I thought would go away once I got away from my mother. But the pain did not go away, so I started going to COA, Children of Alcoholics. They introduced me to "God", so I started my search.

This nice man I was dating introduced me to him three years later. What Dave was doing dating me is beyond me, because he was a Christian, and I was still partying. Dave tells people my language was so bad that I used to embarrass mechanics and truck drivers. I knew I wanted the peace Dave had and I knew I would lose him if I didn't get it, because I was unable to carry on a relationship with a man in my own strength. I would soon run, like I had several times before.

I was sitting in my living room, talking to a God I did not know, telling him I needed to know if he was for real. Jesus spoke to my spirit at that moment and said "Yes, and I am here with you now". Soon after, I called Dave, and he led me to the Lord over the phone. I felt like the monkey had crawled down off my back. Praise God! I finally met Jesus, but I did not have a relationship with him yet. I don't know which is more exciting.

Dave and I had been dating for three months at that point, when I was baptized. Eight months later, we were married. We had his girls, Kristen and Angie, from a previous marriage, every weekend. They were good girls, four and six years old. We went through the usual "You're not my mommy" stuff, but Dave supported me and we got along fine. The hardest part was the emotional trauma the girls were going through. They did not know their mother was a drug addict. They did not understand why she would not be home when we took them home on Sunday night, or maybe she would be asleep and not wake up; or why she would show up two hours late when she was supposed to pick them up. Dave and I did not know either, but we had our suspicions.

We knew we had a real problem when the neighbors called us to tell us the girls were there after school because mommy wasn't home, several times. Then Kristen's report card showed she had missed thirty-eight days of school in the first grade, and was late almost as many days. Finally, the mortgage company foreclosed on her house. They called the police when they found drugs while removing her things. We were there when they arrived. One and a half years after my husband and I married, we had custody of the girls, now six and eight.

I finished school and was working full time as an Engineer. We started a distributorship and ran hard. We achieved some level of success and then "sat back on our laurels" whatever those are. We didn't get rich financially. We did, however, get rich in relationships with each other and with God.

Times were hard during visitation by the girls' mother. One year, during a time of supervised visitation requirements, the girls only saw her every three or four months. Other times, it was a major adjustment when they would come home from being with her, having fun, to being with us, living 'life'.

When I was thirty-two, my mother passed away. I was able to share the gospel with her and pray with her before she died. Only God knows her heart.

By the time Kristen, our oldest, was thirteen, she was in full-blown rebellion, and I was in full- blown depression. I also had a severe weight problem…three hundred pounds - not on me, but on my husband. I just made it _my_ problem. I was in emotional pain from my past, living with sinful thoughts in my heart and my head. I was losing it. My precious mother-in-law would keep telling me she was so proud of me for keeping things together so well. I did on the outside, thank God, but on the inside I was going down hill fast.

The girls were about to get kicked out of Christian school for academic reasons, so we had a meeting with Kristen's teacher. He took one look at me, and said, "You need three books; "The Bondage Breaker", "Grace Walk", and "Victory over the Darkness." He gave me the name of a Christian counseling service and I was on my way. The girls started public school and

I started counseling. Dave and I also decided to try to have a baby.

I spent eight months in counseling with the Holy Spirit. The man I counseled with was what he called 'the facilitator'. He informed me that the real counselor is the Holy Spirit. The counseling was based on forgiveness, renouncing past sins, and replacing the lies I had believed with the truth, God's word. The counselor reminded me over and over that my value is not determined by what my children and my husband do and say, but by my relationship with Christ. I told the counselor of my sinful thoughts. I really wanted out of my marriage. He told me that I could do anything I wanted, that as a Christian, I was free. Then he explained that the reason I am not acting on my desires is because it is not in line with whom I really am, a child of God! Praise God, the truth wins! I was finally getting to <u>know</u> Jesus! I even got rid of my weight problem. I gave it to God!

This is where I learned the importance of memorizing scripture. Every time the devil fires a lie at me, I can cancel it out with the truth. Every time he sends me a sinful thought, I reply with, "I delight in God's law!" Romans 7:22.

A few months after I finished counseling, the devil tried one last tactic. I was so angry with my husband for making what I thought to be a very bad financial decision that I did decide to leave him. The devil actually convinced me that it was a good idea after all. I went to take a shower, and I started thinking about what my relationship with the kids and his parents would be. (I adore his parents, and even though I didn't adore the kids then like I do now, I did love them.)

I got out of the shower, instantly developed a cold, and fell asleep for four hours because Dave gave me 'way too much cough syrup. When I woke up, I realized the attack I had been under and thought, "Wow, what was that? I'm not leaving my husband. I've made a commitment to him and his kids! ". Three weeks later, after a year of trying, God blessed me with the conception of Michael. Four months later, I was able to leave my job.

After two years of public school, the girls were not doing well at all. You could tell by looking at them. We decided to move to the country and home school. Michael was born two weeks after the move. When he was three months old, the girls, now the magic age of fourteen and sixteen, moved in with their mother. The girls had their mom thoroughly convinced that we were tyrants. Fortunately, after years of prayer, their mother had been drug-free for eighteen months at that point. She was rescuing her girls and now had her three-year- old son Tyler to care for as well.

They were gone for almost a year when our fourteen year old, Angie, found out she was pregnant. She knew abortion was inhumane. Our pastor counseled her on adoption. She chose to keep the child, and as we promised, no matter what her decision, we supported her. Before our sweet Kiara was one-year-old, Kristen, then eighteen, found out she was pregnant. That is when she came back to live with us. We now have a handsome one-year-old grandson and a beautiful two-year-old granddaughter.

Angie and Kiara still live with Angie's mother. Angie is finishing high school parallel with a nursing program. Her mother has now been clean for five years, is gainfully employed, has her own home, her own car, is a leader in the Narcotics Anonymous program, and is doing great. Kristen and Tyreese are still living with us and Kristen has recently been blessed with a college scholarship! Praise God!

I found out, through counseling, that love and forgiveness are decisions. You decide to "cancel the debt", and then the feelings will follow. A wise man once told me, "You let your feeler catch up with your doer". If you let your decisions follow your feelings, then you are putting yourself in charge, instead of God. Make your decisions based on his word, and then you will "feel" peace, joy, self-control, and all the rest.

I found out too, that God's forgiveness is real whether I believe it or not! The counselor asked me if I felt like God had forgiven me for the abortion. I said, "Sure, it says so in his word". He asked me if I forgave myself. I said, "No."

He then asked me what made my standards higher than God's. Instant freedom in ten seconds…Wow! Beating ourselves up, or not forgiving one's self, is wasted emotional energy, because it's not true. It is a lie. We are forgiven, whether we "feel" like it or not! No shame allowed!

I would not trade places with anyone. I do not know any of these things without the help of the Holy Spirit. Thanks be to God for allowing my pre-Christian sins to be such an intoxicating blur that I can hardly remember them. It is like these things happened to someone else, mainly because they did, the old me. I am a new creature. Thank you Jesus.

God is Good, all the time. My husband and I have a 'God blessed relationship'. He is my best friend on earth. I don't always like him, and he doesn't always like me. But we always love each other. I am so grateful to him for introducing me to Jesus.

Humanism

"The wisdom of men is foolishness to God."

One cannot be a humanist and a Christian because the beliefs are opposite. The Humanist Manifesto is shocking to a Christian. Here are some points to ponder. "There is no God. Science is god. Man has no soul. There is no heaven or hell. Religion is alien to the intellectual. There is no life after death. No one has the truth. Ethics are situational. Man is a result of evolution. Matter is eternal."

These people refuse to acknowledge that before Darwin died, he repented and renounced his theory of evolution. The foundation for their belief is a myth.

Why would anyone want to adopt such a belief system? Was life so painful they have no hope of something better? Do they not know God loves them? Did they hear a gospel that condemned them?

How can a Christian reach a humanist with the truth? The Word of God is a double-edged sword, dividing the soul from the spirit. Use the Word as God leads you.

Does Everyone Have a Master?

In the old days in America, slaves were brought here to pick cotton and do the hard labor required that white men just could not do as well, especially in the southern states, When these slaves had children, the children were considered property, owned by the slave owner.

When the emancipation of slaves came about, the former owners did not take well to the loss. It meant they would no longer be able to maintain the lifestyle to which they had become accustomed. Many were very wealthy, and therefore had a lot of power. The slaves were often chased down and recaptured, in spite of the law that had set them free.

We all have a spiritual master. Matthew 6:24 says "No man can serve two masters; for either he will hate the one, and love the other; or else he will hold to the one, and despise the other."

We are free to choose which one. Jesus spoke to certain rulers, saying their father was the devil. God gave Adam (man) authority to rule the earth. Adam abdicated it to Satan, turning over the entire race. Adam's offspring automatically became subjects of this spirit being, the same way slaves' children became property of the owner. Jesus had to die to buy us back, and restore His original plan.

Satan takes his job seriously. When we give allegiance to Jesus Christ, our creator, the devil does not take it lightly. The devil chases after us in ways we may not expect. Jesus warned this would happen, and helps us overcome. We win, if we trust God. Sadly, some get confused and return to their former master, who treats them even worse than he did when he was their master the first time.

Jesus said Satan comes to steal, kill, and destroy but Jesus came to give us an abundant life. This Emancipation Proclamation was signed with His precious blood to set the slaves free, and give them a better life.

Why did not everyone become free when Jesus rose from the dead, proclaiming His power over death? Some are still enslaved by lies in their minds and don't recognize thoughts as deliberate measures of Satan to enslave again into bondage. Some just never heard they have been set free. It is up to us to tell them this marvelous news!

Jesus speaks to us from His Word, and gives us everything we need. It is up to us to transform our minds into this new way of thinking so we can remain free, and know what we have been given.

Jesus offers us complete freedom, power over Satan in every way, and even gives us offensive weapons to use against him, found in Ephesians 6. We can use our weapons to live in victory, so we will remain faithful. I John 5 says the evil one does not touch us. So enjoy your freedom and pass on the good news!

He Paid It All
Judy Parrott

Loie told me about living with her children in a haunted house. She swore the canned goods slid off the kitchen closet shelf and crashed onto the floor from time to time with nobody near them, and claimed other things moved about. She would wake in the morning and find the dog's food bowl in weird places and nobody was around. I was fascinated by her strange poltergeist stories, but didn't really believe them.

Loie and I had gone to grade school together. Then I lost track of her until long after I was married when she moved into my neighborhood. She was lonely with her kids in school, so she stopped by for coffee now and then.

After a while it became her daily habit to come by to visit. I was in college and raising three children, and time was precious, but I didn't want to hurt her feelings. It was becoming a real burden and study time was diminishing.

Whenever we went places together, she hung on me, hugged and kissed my cheek, and it became embarrassing to me. In the car one day, I got up the courage to tell her people might misunderstand. I didn't mean to insult her. She was so offended she opened the car door going sixty, and nearly jumped out! I quickly apologized, but after that I kept my distance, realizing there was something terribly amiss.

Loie finally understood the gospel enough to pray with me to invite Jesus into her heart. She was ecstatic with her newfound faith in God. After she prayed for forgiveness, that night God showed her a vivid dream in which Jesus was hanging on the cross naked, and looked like a piece of red meat up there, with no resemblance to a human being. She felt His blood fall on her head as she bowed beneath that cross, and knew He had died in her place. I saw such a change in her, and her fear of being alone decreased, giving me badly needed breathing room.

One day she was visiting while I caught up on my ironing, discussing the Bible, when suddenly her demeanor grew dark. She started accusing me of fanaticism for believing as I did, though I simply trusted God's Word. Her face became red with fury, and she said in a low guttural voice that I was insane for thinking Jesus was going to take me to heaven. Then she laughed at me, a hideous howl that put shudders down my spine! I knew I was suddenly in the presence of something sinister and evil beyond anything human. I didn't know where to turn, and felt like I was in danger of being physically attacked by this large six-foot tall woman now looming over my five-foot-three frame.

I remembered hearing on TV that we have authority over Satan, so I quickly yelled over her terrifying voice, "Satan, I bind you in the name of Jesus!" To my amazement, Loie fell with a loud thump to the floor and started violently convulsing! I was terrified, and figured she might be dying!

My mentor, Marilyn, answered the phone, thank God, and was able to pray for both of us. The convulsions stopped and Loie simply fell asleep on the floor. I covered her with a blanket and left her there, afraid to rouse her. An hour later she woke up, totally unaware of anything that happened!

Soon after that scary demonstration, Marilyn and two friends invited Loie over for a prayer session to relieve her of the scars of a very traumatic past. She had opened up to our prayer group over the few weeks after her salvation experience, and her deep secrets had finally festered to the surface. Loie and several siblings had been raised in severe dysfunction by a mother who was later declared insane and taken to live in a mental institution. As a child, Loie's mother had done unthinkable things to her, inside and outside. One time, she stabbed a fork deep into this small child's upper leg and it stuck there until someone got it out. We wept with compassion as she shared what hell life had been for her.

The day came that Loie was ready to let go of her past and the oppression that was still tormenting her and giving her nightmares. Marilyn, Trudy and Clark had been fasting for Loie in preparation for the battle about to ensue. Loie came in and sat down in the easy chair ready for prayer. Marilyn began, and the Holy Spirit was present to lead Loie to freedom.

The struggle lasted over four hours! As God revealed the names of spirits and rebuked them one at a time, Loie tried to lunge at Marilyn, but she quickly said, "I bind your arms to that chair in Jesus' name!" Loie said later she was firmly locked in that chair by some invisible force. God brought scriptures to their minds to pray, and revealed one spirit after another. At one point Loie tried kicking the women so they all moved behind her while they prayed. Her eyes darted back and forth glaring with unveiled hatred as the spirits fought to remain, but were unable to resist the name of King Jesus and His mighty blood.

Finally the battle ended. All four were exhausted but greatly relieved. Loie was free for the first time since she was a small child. All through her life she had dealt with her own uncontrollable behavior, followed by terrible punishment and abuse. It wasn't her fault. The Bible says the sins of the fathers visit the children, to the third and fourth generation, and it was certainly true in this case.

Some teach that a Christian cannot have a demon. Evil spirits cannot possess the spirit of a believer, but they certainly can torment them in other ways, and Loie was evidence of that. How many are still tormented but unable to heal because of false beliefs? The demons laugh as people live with them and try to find peace. It helps to have a support system with such situations and find people they trust to be honest with. They need to believe the Word of God and obey it, take authority over the devil and submit to God.

Colossians 1:13 (KJV) *Who hath delivered us from the power of darkness, and hath translated* us *into the kingdom of his dear Son.*

1976 (The Holy Spirit brought this to me as a spiritual three-year-old.)

The following conversation is inspiration from the Spirit. I hope they will speak to your heart as well. We are just one body, after all.

"My Child, You need again my words of comfort. I sense your pain, your embarrassment, and your bewilderment. Do not dismay, for I have told you I will not leave you. I know your heart. You do not have yet the strength to do all that I ask of you, but do not be disheartened. The long walk has just begun. The journey at its end will have taught you many great things. What do you wish of me- that I would heal your wounds? First they must remain open to the air so they do not fester. As they are exposed, then healing will begin.

It is true that you see yourself in a worse state than before. My light is exposing for you what was previously in darkness. Gradually the light seeps into corners previously hidden to you. Would you prefer the darkness to return or would you wish the light to remain, purifying that area as does the sun on a germ?"

DEMONS MUST FLEE

Gigi screamed when she saw the black furry thing climb up Tom's back, onto his shoulder, and jump out into the darkness. What was it? We had our eyes closed praying, but we all realized something had left the room.

Tom had been imprisoned by a drug habit since he was thirteen. We even moved from Michigan to Georgia partly to get him out of the environment we could not control. It did no good. Within a few weeks, he was entrenched with a new group of users, and they introduced him to the real stuff-cocaine. He was seventeen when we moved.

He was always kind and gentle and would do anything for anyone. He hasn't changed.   People could walk all over him, and he would never say a cruel word to anyone. I have seen him stoned only once. He was twenty, and called me at two A.M. He said he was stoned on cocaine and didn't know if he could make it home, so he was going to sleep in his car in the ghetto downtown.

I urged him to get home any way he could, as soon as it wore off enough to drive. If he stayed, he might never come home alive. He agreed, and I began to pray like I never prayed before. God is so good. He gave me peace and the ability to praise Him in this awful situation. Tom had never admitted his drug use to me until that night.

He arrived home within an hour. I was sitting on the front porch steps waiting. He parked his old car on a hill that curves off our driveway and came to sit next to me. I gave him a hug. What else could I do at this point? We sat down. I put my hands on his arm and prayed for his deliverance. His arm muscles were violently contracting with each heartbeat, but the jerking subsided. We heard a creaking noise and stared while his car slowly began to roll backward down the hill toward the house at the bottom of the cul de sac!

His emergency brake broke and the car was picking up speed. Tom ran, but he couldn't catch the car before it slammed into a power box at the edge of our yard. Thank God it stopped, but the power box was emitting sparks and making scary noises. Lights were flashing off and on in the houses around us! Someone must have called the power company because they were there in just a few minutes. Tom got a whopping fine and had to repair his car at his own expense.

This story began with Gigi. Let me tell you about her. She was Tom's second wife. He met her while in a Teen Challenge rehab center in Chattanooga. They had married and he was doing very well for over a year. Then the drug dealers found him again, and before long he was hooked, after a year and a half in treatment!

Gigi had already evicted him, and he had been jailed more than once. He got out on bail, and was to be sentenced for at least a year in prison. Gigi asked if there was anything that could be done to help him. I called a couple good friends and we began to fast and pray for three days. Tom agreed to meet us, with Gigi, the day before his court date.

Gay Smith, Mark, my husband and I met them there. Tom looked really awful, and Gigi was so worried. Mark was so kind and had such wisdom. He asked Gigi if she knew anything about the baptism in the Holy Spirit, and she didn't. So he patiently went through all the scriptures pertaining to this experience of power from God. When he was finished, Gigi, a Christian, asked Jesus to fill her in His Holy Spirit. All of a sudden, we heard strange words coming from her mouth, and we were all as amazed as she was!

Mark has been mightily used by God in this area of ministry over the years. He suggested we simply stand in a circle and praise God in our prayer language, because "praise breaks the yoke of bondage". This is perfect praise, so we could not go wrong.

We must have sounded like a bunch of wild crazy people but we did not care. We were desperate at this point to see this enslaved man set free. Tom had also been baptized in the Holy Ghost a couple years before, in Teen Challenge.

We had prayed about ten minutes when suddenly Tom broke down weeping, "It's gone!" It was then that Gigi exclaimed that she saw this black furry thing like an ugly monkey slither up Tom's back and onto his shoulder and jump off. She didn't see where it went, but it disappeared.

We were so excited for Tom and couldn't get over what Gigi had seen. I had never heard of seeing a demon before, but we were all convinced this had to be what it was! We prayed a while longer and thanked God for His deliverance. Mark shared many scriptures with Tom to help encourage him to maintain his freedom and stay in the Word.

The next morning Tom and I went to the court together, after praying again that the Lord would have mercy and have His way. The judge brought Tom forward to talk to him. He told him a story that still astounds me. All Tom's records had been lost! The judge had to release him because there was no paper trail to prove his case! Smart move! Is God not the most awesome attorney you have ever seen? Hallelujah! We gave Him all the glory!

Leviticus 26:8
And five of you shall chase an hundred, and an hundred of you shall put ten thousand to flight: and your enemies shall fall before you by the sword.

Luke 10:19
Behold, I give unto you power to tread on serpents and scorpions, and over all the power of the enemy: and nothing shall by any means hurt you.

John 14:12
Verily, verily, I say unto you, He that believeth on me, the works that I do shall he do also; and greater works than these shall he do; because I go unto my Father.

Matthew 21:22
And all things, whatsoever ye shall ask in prayer, believing, ye shall receive.

Mark 16:15-20
And he said unto them, Go ye into all the world, and preach the gospel to every creature. [16]He that believeth and is baptized shall be saved; but he that believeth not shall be damned. [17]And these signs shall follow them that believe; In my name shall they cast out devils; they shall speak with new tongues; [18]They shall take up serpents; and if they drink any deadly thing, it shall not hurt them; they shall lay hands on the sick, and they shall recover.

Bondage Breaker

Scripture Focus: Psalm 107:20 *He sent his word, and healed them, and delivered them from their destructions.*

The Holy Spirit reminds me of this whenever I feel bondage in my life, Even a diet does not work for me unless I combine choices with the power of God's promises. His word is mighty to the pulling down of strongholds. Temptations become ropes that bind me unless I let His truth set me free.

I found some sword scriptures that are making a big difference in this struggle when I speak them aloud and put my trust in them. Romans 6:11: Likewise reckon ye also yourselves to be dead indeed unto sin, but alive unto God through Jesus Christ our Lord. I Corinthians 10:13: There hath no temptation taken you but such as is common to man: but God *is* faithful, who will not suffer you to be tempted above that ye are able; but will with the temptation also make a way to escape, that ye may be able to bear *it.* Revelation 12:11 [11] And they overcame him by the blood of the Lamb, and by the word of their testimony; and they loved not their lives unto the death.

Prayer: Dear Lord, Thank you for the power of your words to deliver me from the lusts of my flesh. Help me to always trust not in my own ability, but in your word alone.

Inspiration during prayer

"Please do not despair. Let your confession be positive. Give the enemy no grip to hold onto. Allow him no space in your testimony. You are a peculiar people. Did I promise the world would love you as their own? No, but you will suffer much as I did in this alien place. It is not always pleasant, is it?

But even this works out for good. It demands that you seek me and yearn for a deeper walk with me wherein you would have greater protection from the barbs which shall be hurled at you for my sake."

A Spirit called Cancer
By Sylvia Swegle

The enemy has tried unsuccessfully over my lifetime to extinguish my life. When I was six years old, a pair of thick scissors penetrated my chin area and missed my jugular vein. When I was seven years old I contacted pneumonia, and the physician informed my mom if I lived through the night, I would survive. When I was eight years old, a little boy pushed me one story down into a coal storage basement where I struck the side of my face into a thick cement floor and my chin burst open.

When I was about twenty years old a catamaran that I was sailing in on a vacation to the Bahamas capsized and I was thrown out into water I found out later was shark infested. I clung to the side of the boat until help arrived—six hours later.

In my thirties, while driving down Bethany Home Road, a man pulled out from a little street and flew into my path. I braked, and my car spun around 180 degrees and I was literally facing three lanes of traffic coming towards me. The list goes on and on. So you can see there has been a mighty power preventing death from striking me down.

As much as I knew about the schemes of the enemy to destroy me, I let my guard down over the last several months. Feeling hopeless and despondent about my life and how much I have grieved the Lord with my waywardness, I became angry and bitter about my life but directed it toward God.

Finally, I expressed my sadness by confessing my thoughts out loud that I would like to die. I saw no reason for life; rather, I saw many times where I did not glorify God by my actions. As the months went on, my depression caused a heavier and heavier heart. My husband saw how I acted one day and then be overcome with depression the next.

The enemy loves to hear this; he found a way in. A dark grayness encamped within me and I felt as though I was dragging around a weighted ball. Everything was so hard to do--which made the whole situation worse.

I was preparing for my yearly bladder exam for previous cancer that I had been healed from. I decided if they discovered cancer again, I would not fight it; I would not tell my husband and I would let it run its course--to death. So I was surprised but not surprised when the doctor who examined me said I had cancer--again. This time, it appeared it was worse than before, and only one year had gone by.

I knew instantly what had brought this into existence--my own negative thinking and confessions. I changed my mind and decided to let my husband know.

His encouraging words were that we would fight it again. In my shock, I contacted my friend Janice, and before I could reach my other friend, Dee, she called and found out, too.

At this point, I still did not feel like fighting for my life, but Dee said something that I wrote down: "You must choose life." But did I want to choose life?

Janice started the spiritual ball rolling by contacting everyone in the FFF (Foundation

Fellowship Family) and beyond, and from that point forward God's mercy was put into action.

Bessie, our dear friend, wrote and had a word regarding unforgiveness. As I read her note, I realized that I had bitterness towards God. He was the first one I came to, regarding all the hurtful things I said to Him--the One who died on the cross for me, loves me unconditionally and has never broken His covenant with me.

I didn't realize that behind the scenes God was working some amazing "coincidences". Janice's church group was praying for me. She was conversing with Bessie and felt I needed deliverance. I agreed it would be in order. Another friend found I was diagnosed with cancer and she cried out to the Lord and asked what she could do for me. She remembered the evening that week she had dinner with a couple and had asked the Lord to help her be open to what He had in store for her with them. The husband at dinner was talking to her about the healing he had received. "Healing?" she asked.

Yes, he had been healed from a sore shoulder. She kept asking him about who healed him and where it occurred. The man handed her a business card for Hardcore Christianity. The Lord brought this to her memory, so she sent me the information on their Sunday healing service.

Mind you, I had gone to the urologist on Thursday. By Friday I had the healing service information. I had examined myself for any unforgiveness after Bessie wrote, and was ready to attend the Sunday healing service. Amazing! God does fast work.

Vern and I drove off to the healing service that we thought started at 4 pm. When we arrived at 3:45 pm, we were informed it actually started at 4:30 pm. Vern and I sat in our car as he looked up scriptures that Dee gave me. I expected it to be a service in which people might come up front to have someone pray for them, or the pastor might call out to the audience that certain diseases were being healed.

Rather, the 4:30 pm session was individualized. I went into a room with a counselor, whereupon I told him I was a

Christian for 35 years. I then shared the rest of my story.

He asked me, "When was the last time you heard from the Holy Spirit?" Well, it was while I was in the auditorium talking with God. The auditorium shows scriptures on the wall to prepare you to receive from God and to confess any unforgiveness. The counselor asked the question that I wasn't sure how to answer: "Do you want to live"?

Within me I felt I should tell him "No", but instead, what came out of my lips was "Yes, of course I want to live". And so began my deliverance.

The counselor recognized the spirits from parts of my story: spirit of cancer, hopelessness, suicide and lies. As we commanded the spirits that they had no authority over me, I grew more and more exhausted. The counselor kept encouraging me to command the named spirit to leave my body. It seemed like an eternity before the spirit of cancer exited with my lips peeled back and my teeth bared like a snarling wolf. The counselor insisted there were more demons of cancer, and we continued on. Eventually I was coughing and spitting up (into a bucket) with the last demon resisting but leaving, realizing the counselor was determined to continue commanding its exit.

The counselor moved on to the demons; then laid hands on my stomach and commanded any cancer to leave my body. When we were finished, I stood up, and that heavy weight was lifted off my body as well as the grayness. I saw the schemes of the enemy and that he is determined to kill, steal, and destroy us.

Vern was in the room while the deliverance occurred, and while praying, wrote down what I was experiencing. It is recorded. Vern was my witness as to what took place. He acknowledged that I definitely needed deliverance after what he saw.

It made believers out of us! The doctor checked me after the deliverance, and proclaimed I am free of cancer! Praise God forever!

Freedom from Bondage

"Stand fast therefore in the liberty wherewith Christ has made us free." Ephesians 5:11

Most of us are shocked to learn that we have been exposed to the occult (meaning hidden or secret things) during our lives. When I was a child, my relatives used to entertain themselves by "table tipping", having no idea they were dabbling in the occult!

See if you or anyone in your family history has been involved unaware. It is easy to repent and be free of any effects.

HAVE YOU EVER;

    A. Had your fortune told by use of cards, tealeaves, palm reading, etc.?

    B. Read or followed horoscopes?

    C. Been hypnotized, or done yoga?

    D. Attended a séance or spiritualist meeting?

    E. Had a "life or reincarnation reading"?

    F. Consulted a ouija board, planchette, cards, crystal ball- for fun, out of curiosity, or in earnest?

    G. Played with so-called "games" of an occult nature, such as E.S.P., Telepathy, Kabala, etc?

    H. Consulted a medium?

    I. Sought healing through magic conjuring and charming, through a spiritualist, Christian

Scientist, or anyone who
practices "spirit-healing"?

J. Sought to locate missing
objects or persons by
consulting someone who has
psychic powers?

K. Practiced table-lifting,
levitation, or automatic
writing?

L. Practiced water-witching?

M. Been given a charm of any kind
for protection?

N. Read or possessed occult or
spiritualist literature- such as:
books on astrology, interpretation
of dreams, metaphysics, religious
cults, self-realization, fortune-
telling, magic, ESP, clairvoyance,
psychic phenomena, and especially
such occult magical books as
"Secrets of the Psalms", and the
so-called "Sixth and Seventh
books of Moses"?

O. Taken LSD?

P. Possessed any occult or pagan
religious objects?

Q. Had your handwriting
analyzed, practiced mental

suggestion, cast a magic spell,
or sought psychic experiences?
R. Practiced transcendental
meditation?

FORBIDDEN BY SCRIPTURE

All forms of fortune telling, spiritism, magic practices, and any involvement in false religious cults are absolutely forbidden by Scripture. God condemns both practice and participation in them:
Exodus 22:18
Deuteronomy 18:9-12
Leviticus 19: 26, 31
Leviticus 20:6,27
I Chronicles 10:13-14
Isaiah 8:19
Jeremiah 27:9-10
Zechariah 10:2
Malachi 3:5
Acts 8:9-13
Acts 16:16-18
Acts 19:19
Galatians 5:16-21
Revelation 21:8

Revelation 22:14,15 Blessed are those who wash their robes, that they may have the right to the tree of life and may go through the gates into the city. Outside are the dogs, those who practice magic arts, the sexually immoral, the murderers, the idolaters and everyone who loves and practices falsehood.

Occult involvement breaks the first commandment, and invokes God's curse: Ex. 20:3-5.

THE DOOR MUST BE CLOSED BY YOU.

Those who have been involved in occultism have opened a "door" of access to oppressing spirits which they themselves must close by positive action and faith on their part.

A. It is impossible for a TRUE Christian's SPIRIT to be possessed by any other spirit but the Holy Spirit – but Christians have personalities which may be opened to satanic powers through occult involvement.

B. Occult oppression and subjection always results from an individual's involvement in some form of the before-mentioned practices by involvement as a practitioner, as a subject, follower, or participant.

C. Some symptoms of oppression or subjection are: inability to read and study the Bible; uncontrollable evil thoughts; blasphemous thoughts about the Trinity when trying to pray; self-pity; fear; uncontrollable temper; unrelenting anxiety; lying; hate; uncontrollable emotions; resistance to spiritual things; religious delusions; depression; pain; apathy; disease; compulsive thoughts of suicide, etc...

METHOD OF DELIVERANCE
a. Confession of faith in Christ: "Lord Jesus, I accept you as the Messiah, the Christ, the Son of God. I know your Blood was shed that I might be set free. Thank you, Jesus, for your blood that sets me free." Even if you have already done this once in your life, renew this confession of faith at this time. It is essential.

b. Confession of occult sins: All occult involvement must be confessed if liberation is to be realized. Make a confession similar to the following: "Father, in Jesus' name, I confess that I have sinned against you, and your Word, by doing (tell God each thing on the list:)

> NOTE: If you possess any magic charms, religious or occult books, Objects, and so on, they should be burned immediately after confession.

c. Denunciation of Satan and command him to depart:

> This must be a direct command to Satan himself. For example: "Satan, I hereby renounce you and all your works in my life. I command you, in Jesus' name, to depart and trouble me no more. I by an act of my will, close the door to you forever."

> > a. Ask God to fill these now empty areas with the Holy Spirit:

> "Lord Jesus, I give you my entire body, soul, and spirit. Please fill me with the Holy Spirit, that I may follow You."

What must we do to stay free?

> You play a part in 'working out your salvation with great respect' to the One who can keep you free,

> Matthew 12:43-45
> Acts. 19: 18-20.

Study the scriptures:

> Romans 10:17

Learn what God says about deliverance, and how Jesus' name helps you:

> Psalm 91
> Exodus 12:23
> Romans 8:28-39
> Revelation 12:11
> Luke 10:1
> Mark 16:17
> John 10:27-29
> Isaiah 54:11-
> Ephesians 2:6-8; 6:10-18

Talk to Jesus as your best friend. He knows your heart and loves you the most.

Luke 18:1; Acts 2:41-47

Resisting bondage

Ephesians 4:27; Do not give the devil a foothold. (Avoid any activity that gives him permission.)

James 4:7 …and be not entangled again with the yoke of bondage. (Overcome evil practices with the opposite-replace bad with good.)
Gal. 5:1 It is for freedom that Christ has set us free. Stand firm, then, and do not let yourselves be burdened again by a yoke of slavery.

(Parts taken from "Reference material Guidance Guidelines" tract)

As you can see, I believe the only way to freedom from drugs or any other control is with God and His mighty power against Satan, who is a real angel, and is the enemy of God and those who follow Him. Once Satan is involved with our lives, only God is more powerful than an angel. God promised to fight for us and defend and protect us. He does a great job!

I hope this has helped you. I have searched for promises from God's Word, because I know He cannot lie, and I can trust Him to do what He promised. So I remind Him of what He said daily, and I surrender these 'prisoners' into His care. When I take my hands off them, and give them to Him, I am not allowed to worry any more, but just thank Him for what He is doing in their lives. It is our faith that justifies us in God's eyes.

God got into my hands some old Kenneth Hagin deliverance tapes that are so helpful. He talks about being in the spirit in a way I did not know about. 'In the spirit' means surrounded by that Shekinah glory like in the OT. It is all about Jesus- not us. We cannot muster any of this. It is up to God- the timing, the guidance, everything. He knows our hearts and responds to them. Praise God. We are getting close to freedom- from these sicknesses, from drug addiction, the works!

Inspiration

Let no fear overtake you. I am not a source of fear, but of love, power and a sound mind. What is the definition of a sound mind? Consider this truth.

I give you joy. Bask in it. Enjoy it. Return to it when the world tries to hurt you, or rejects your message of truth.

I know your motives. The world does not understand. Do you see the pain that my disciples felt? Their own people rejected them. Their families laughed at them. They did not have to defend me. I need no defending. To defend another, you must be stronger than that one. Are you stronger than the Almighty? It is enough for you to simply glimpse at me now and then through natural beauty to know that I am Almighty. Do I need defending?

The Visitation
Jeff B.

Until now, I have not told many people about this, but I realized someone might need to hear this story. For about two years, a spirit visited me. It was shaped like a man; it had no face and wore a black robe with a hood. It would come in while I was awake or sometimes wake me from sleep, try to hold me down and suffocate me.

At first I was afraid and tried to fight it. I tried to talk to it, but nothing ever worked. It never spoke; it only watched me. Whatever it was, it had a strong evil presence. I could tell it was there even when I couldn't see it.

I remember one time I was searching the Internet trying to find out what it was, and the front door came flying open while I was in the middle of reading an article. For the longest time I would ignore it, and try convincing myself it was just my imagination. Then it began to come more frequently, not only at home, but also at work, school, and the gym. My girlfriend said she saw it, and was going to leave me because of it.

Something had to be done. I refused to keep living in such a manner. Right before I made the decision to check myself into a mental hospital, I saw a sermon on T.V. The evangelist spoke of demons and how Jesus Christ gave us power over them through His name. He said, "Rebuke them in the name of Jesus Christ."

So the next time the demon attacked me, I said to it, "In the name of Jesus Christ I rebuke you." It left immediately, but it came back three weeks later. I did the same thing again, rebuking it in Jesus' name.

A few months went by before it showed up again. Then after a year it appeared. Each time I rebuked it in the name of Jesus. There is power in the name of Jesus that makes demons tremble. Nowadays I'm no longer afraid; I don't believe I'm crazy, and demons no longer bother me.

2 Timothy 1:7 (KJV)_*For God hath not given us the spirit of fear; but of power, and of love, and of a sound mind.*

Blessings and Curses

The Chinese have a reputation as people in general who revere their ancestors. Americans, on the other hand, pay much less attention to their roots than the Chinese. It may be a mistake.

Derek Prince, a prominent Bible teacher, reveals things from the Bible that would shock most Christians. As a matter of fact, most will never accept most of what he teaches because it is so radical. However, he teaches nothing that is not from the mouth of God Himself.

Derek made a list of seven indications of a curse; they correspond to the curses in Deut. 28. They are not always originating from our ancestors. Sometimes we have been involved with something that has resulted in curses. We must examine our hearts often. It is a wicked tricky world out there.

This brilliant man has written many books on inner healing and of the spirit realm. One that would help us live victoriously is called, "Blessing or Curse." It is quite an eye opener.

He said we are products of our past more than we know. It influences much in our lives, and what our ancestors got into passes on.

The word *blessing* occurs in the Bible about 410 times, and the word *curse* about 230 times. Everything in the Bible is of utmost importance. What is a blessing and what is a curse? How can we recognize a curse operating in us? How do we revoke it and release ourselves from its consequences? How can we receive the blessings of God?

Some possible symptoms of a need for deliverance or repentance for one's self or ancestors:

1.Mental and/ or emotional breakdown, trembling heart, anxious mind
2.Repeated or chronic sicknesses (esp. hereditary)
3.Barrenness or tendency to miscarry, related female problems
4.Breakdown of marriage, and family alienation
5.Continuing financial insufficiency
6.Being 'accident-prone'
7. A history of suicides and unnatural untimely deaths

One needs to do some detective work to find the source of problems. It is not difficult for a Christian to break the power of such curses, but he must understand his position of authority that results from being a child of God. We were saved with words spoken from our heart, and we are also set free with words.

Generational Bondage

Years ago, the US court did not convene until those in office had cleansed their hearts of all evil and sin, repented and got their hearts right with God. They spent time in corporate prayer before each session. Satan has made inroads in America that threaten our peace and safety. Removing prayer from schools was a huge blow.

You may be able to relate, and may even be involved with the witchcraft that is wreaking havoc in many families. Those with a pure heart will be able to confront the demons and kick them out. How do we get a pure heart?

We repent of all known sin, pray God reveals unknown or hidden sin, and we ask forgiveness of each other for things we have held against each other. It can't hurt to fast a few days from the lusts of our flesh and seek God with a whole heart. He will forgive us and set us free.

We all probably have generational curses to deal with. I have family sin, an alcoholic grandfather and other sins we know nothing about, though most of the family on both sides were definitely Christian people. That garbage plus our own family garbage may be a key for whatever holds our precious grandson Chandler in bondage to a brain disorder.

We need to learn about them if possible by keeping no secrets. We must each repent for our sins and those of our ancestors. This can be done while together or alone with God. God said if we would repent, turn from our wicked ways, He is just and will forgive us our sins and cleanses us from all unrighteousness.

Everyone in a family suffers from the sins of a few, but there are none righteous. We all need to get a purified heart so we can all be free of demonic influences. God told Cain that sin crouches at the door, waiting to devour him. It still does it today. But now we have the blood of Jesus backing us up, just like a cop has a judge backing up his authority and giving him power to put criminals into bondage.

None can come to throw stones at the other's sins. We must all be concerned with our own sin and being free of it before we can take the splinter out of anybody's eye.

You will know the Truth and the Truth shall set you free. The Bible says to expose the deeds of darkness.

Mark 16:16-20 (KJV)

He that believeth and is baptized shall be saved; but he that believeth not shall be damned.

[17] And these signs shall follow them that believe; In my name shall they cast out devils; they shall speak with new tongues;

[18] They shall take up serpents; and if they drink any deadly thing, it shall not hurt them; they shall lay hands on the sick, and they shall recover.

Delivered Due to a Dream

My mom lost my dad, her only partner from her youth. He was 72. Six weeks after he died, a grieving neighbor consoled her. His wife had just died. But he was an alcoholic and not a Christian.

He and Mom started dating a bit. I was staying with her. One night I had a terrible dream. In an attempt to stop the bleeding of their souls, having both been spiritually cut in half, two (only in the dream) had become one. In my dream, they joined together momentarily. I saw half of my mom and half of that man, both cut in half, pressing the halves together to make a while person. Weird. Can you imagine one side of a woman and one side of a man divided in half, pressing the halves together to stop the bleeding?

The bleeding stopped for a time, but since they did not line up exactly, they separated again. The scab ripped away, leaving each of them in worse shape than they were before.

God revealed this to me, I know. I believe it revealed the presence of evil spirits that have come to bring trouble. They would be legally allowed to come into her because she was about to disobey God. One is named a *seducing spirit* and the other is named *lying spirit*. God told me their names in the dream.

I told Mom my dream the next morning, and she was shocked, like I was. Mom agreed we needed to pray, so we took authority over these demons and cast them out. They had to leave. They had no legal ground to remain since the blood of Jesus has been applied, and they had no power over Mom.

Mom finally found the man God saved for her, seven years later when she was 78. An old boyfriend from her teens lost his wife. Mom saw it in the paper and invited him for coffee. Within a year they were married! They enjoyed each other greatly for ten years until she died at 88 and he died a year later.

A Special Delivery

My knees trembled strangely when my husband introduced me to Janet, a young woman who had come to him from Michigan to Georgia for a job interview. I met her that evening, unexpectedly. She had become hysterical in his office, screaming words he could not comprehend. He called our psychologist friend Jim, who was able to calm her down. She shakily left Roger's office for her hotel with Jim's phone number in her purse. (Needless to say, he didn't hire her.)

In the middle of the night, Jim woke us with a problem. "Your friend is out of control again and the hotel wants her to leave." Not knowing what to do, Rog and

Jim met at the hotel and finally decided to bring her to our house. Rog asked if she would like to come meet his wife, and she seemed comforted that she could talk to a woman. God knows why. He brought her home, introduced her to me and went to bed!

We had a peaceful visit about nothing important. I invited her to stay overnight, but as we prepared for bed, she again lost contact with reality, screaming in terror about things she seemed to be seeing. Leading her to the couch, I prayed for God to give her peace. She quietly curled up with my blanket like a baby and closed her eyes, grabbing my hand tightly as though she feared floating away. Sitting on the floor next to her, I held her hand praying under my breath for answers. As long as I was with her, she slept. I dozed off and on during the night with her hand still in mine. She woke up before dawn trembling, shocking me from sleep with a scream, "I have to get saved!"

This was supernatural; I had not mentioned God at all to her. She prayed after me, asking God to forgive her, and invited Jesus to take over her life.

What a transformation there was in this beautiful young woman! We had a wonderful day together, studying the Bible and sharing our life experiences- except for one big secret.

We went to bed that night, and all fell asleep exhausted. At 2AM I sat up in bed hearing Janet screaming into my bedroom, "I am leaving! There are Bibles in this house!" There she stood in our doorway, coat on and purse in hand.

Down the stairs she flew, and out the front door into the night. My knees knocked together so badly, I could hardly pull my slacks on! The room was icy cold all of a sudden for some reason. She was out of her mind, and had no idea where she was. My husband didn't know what to do, so he called 911. Four police cars were there in moments.

In the yard I realized an evil spirit causing great agitation was attacking her, and for some reason it was not submitting to me. The Holy Spirit let me know it was now her responsibility to openly confess Christ to the enemy. I told her she could now use her new authority to resist him. She began screaming at him, "Satan, I now belong to Jesus. I am giving you back your books, your ring, and your cape! She threw something from her finger, but I never found a ring. She had been a Satanist, involved in devil worship!

She refused to get in the car with the policeman, so I rode with her to the mental hospital. My husband followed the police car. Her grandfather, a Presbyterian pastor, drove down a few days later and brought her back to Michigan.

Her grandfather had been praying a long time for her deliverance, and he finally got his answer. Friends of mine in Holland, Michigan, Marilyn again, followed up on her and guided her in her Christian walk. Janet has been doing very well ever since, once she learned what she had inherited from God. Everything!

John 8:36 (KJV) *If the Son therefore shall make you free, ye shall be free indeed.*

How to enter the Kingdom of God and become a Christian:

This is here just in case you missed it. <u>This is the most important page in the whole book!</u> Can a sinner can enter heaven? Aren't we all sinners? What hope do we have?
These steps will explain it.

1. Admit to God you have sinned in your life, like everyone else. Romans 3:23 says, "All have sinned and come short of the glory of God."

2. Believe in your heart that Christ died for your sins and that He rose again the third day from the dead in the flesh. John 3:16 says "God sent his only begotten son, that whoever believes on him shall be saved.

3. Talk to God: It is simple enough for children to understand. We are all children in God's eyes. You can say, Dear Jesus, I choose to believe you became my substitute, died for me and rose again, I call on your name and ask you to save me. Thank you. Amen.

4. Tell someone what you did. Telling a Christian is easiest. Romans 10:9 says, *"If you will confess with your mouth that Jesus is Lord, and believe in your heart that God raised him from the dead, you shall be saved."*

WELCOME TO THE FAMILY OF GOD! YOU HAVE BECOME A NEW CREATURE! OLD THINGS HAVE PASSED AWAY, AND ALL THINGS HAVE BECOME NEW.

Inspiration

"Go now out into the poor world again. Go renewed. Help the poor, heal the brokenhearted with a listening ear, with open love, with prejudice for no one, least of all those most prejudiced against, which are the obese children. They, more than any, need my love. They try to be protected from the pains of this world, but are the most vulnerable. Their armor is more like flypaper than anything.

Love them all, but love me most of all. How do you show your love to me? What could man give a king who already owns everything? He can give his allegiance, his honor, his praise, his possessions, his concerns, and his will. This is love, that he will lay down his life for his friend. What greater love is there than this? But it cannot be done unless his fear of death is conquered. It cannot be done unless he trusts his friend and knows the price is not too high. You see that trust involves many concepts. It is a matter of caring, concern for another which reduces ones' ego to a great degree. It is a concept of individual involvement with the life of someone other than himself.

Have you considered the rarity of this occurrence in our lives? Even with your own offspring, do you really unselfishly give that child your entire self? I think not. Simple resentment over them waking you in the night is an example of selfishness innate in all creatures. There is one in need, but your need supercedes it. Will this tendency ever be broken? Not until you are free of this cumbersome world, free of this body will it ever change. The truth which is in Christ Jesus is the only force which will free you, but it is gradual. Do you know the ancient pattern of Japanese foot-wrapping? A person would experience excruciating pain if the wrappings were all removed at once. So it is with the truth. If I were to reveal your sinful nature to you all at once, you would grieve and suffer terribly to know the whole truth. I must gently replace evil with good. This cushions the shock as I gently unwrap and reveal your true nature to you. I wish to protect you from self-condemnation, which is an evil process. Consider the effects of it in those who grieve their loved ones. It is often disastrous."

An Unwanted Guest

The effect of serving other gods is always devastating. My neighbor, Carla had been studying Transcendental Meditation for quite a while. I was delighted when she agreed to come to church. She had gone forward when the pastor invited those in need of prayer to meet him at the altar. He immediately discerned as God revealed to him that she had a demon tormenting her, and cast a spirit of fear out of her right then! She collapsed on the floor weeping with joy.

Carla accepted Jesus that day. She shared about having lived with crushing terror for years that had escalated after exposure to this type of meditation, which opened her soul to more torment. She thought she was getting closer to God, but she encountered a counterfeit.

An evil spirit can enter a vulnerable person during a crisis. She remembered exactly when it entered her as a child. She was hiding from her father under a table, and was in bondage to fear ever since. She was set free in a moment by prayer! "God has not given us a spirit of fear, but of love and of power, and a sound mind." 2 Timothy 1:7 Jesus came to set the captives free. John 8:36 *"If the Son therefore shall make you free, you shall be free indeed. "Greater is He in you than he that is in the world."* 1 John 4:4 *Ye are of God, little children, and have overcome them: because greater is he that is in you, than he that is in the world. "Nothing shall by any means harm you".* Luke 10:19 *Behold, I give unto you power to tread on serpents and scorpions, and over all the power of the enemy: and nothing shall by any means hurt you.*

The name of Jesus is so mighty and powerful that when this name is spoken, devils all tremble. The devils believe and know who He is. When Jesus told the evil spirits in the demoniac to be still, they were silent. Jesus passed this power on to us. This is our job, and it is necessary to take dominion and set the captives free in Jesus' name! Mark 16:16-18 tells us to cast out demons, preach the gospel, and heal the sick.

We must not let the devil deceive us into being afraid of him. He is afraid of us, and very afraid when he knows that WE know it! Either the Word of God is completely true or none of it is true, whether or not we understand it all. If it is not, we are to be pitied above all men. I vow to you...it is TRUE! I stake my life on it.

Does God Speak to Us?

Many people use in conversation, "The Lord told me..." What does this mean? Does He speak to their ears? Does He put a thought in their mind? Does scripture 'leap out of the page'? Is it valid to say this, or is it presumption?

All we have is our experience and God's Word, the Bible, to validate it. All through the Old Testament, the Lord obviously spoke to men. Adam and God spoke to each other in the Garden of Eden. God spoke clearly to Job during his testing time. The events are too numerous to mention.

But here we are in the New Testament times. Jesus has come and returned to heaven, and sent His Holy Spirit to live within us. Does the Holy Spirit speak to us? If so, how?

All I have is my experience, and this I can share. Since my conversion, I have talked volumes to the Lord, assuming He heard me by faith in His Word. He said, *"Call on me, and I will answer, and show you great and mighty things you know not."* Jeremiah 33:3. In John 10:27 in the N.T., He said, *"My sheep know my voice..."* John

8:47 says he that is of God hears God's words. This can be words of scripture or words spoken to an individual, based on the scripture.

Perhaps God simply 'brings to our remembrance' what we need to know, after we have hidden His word in our hearts. This could be what we sense within and say 'the Lord told me'. He says, "You need no man to teach you, but the Holy Spirit will teach you all things."

I have sensed words in my mind that did not seem to originate from me. I write them down, usually, and test them to see if they come true, or if good comes from them. One day I was in a public laundry, and a woman near me was folding her clothes, looking very angry. I avoided visiting with her, because she didn't look very pleasant. I got in the car to leave, and a strong thought came to my mind," Go tell that woman I love her." I sat a moment, thinking of the logical repercussions of such an act. But to test if it was the Lord, I tried it. She burst out crying, and said she had been praying God would reach her somehow, and let her know He still cared. What a blessing it turned out to be! Is this scriptural? I believe it is. I am His sheep, too.

Usually the Lord shows me He heard my prayer by doing things, rather than speaking. I was driving a car from Michigan to Georgia a few years ago, pulling a 24 foot long houseboat. While driving down a steep mountain in Tennessee, the trailer bolts that held the wheels on loosened up. I lost control and the trailer whipped the car violently from one side of the road to the other. The tire finally worked its way off the trailer, and I watched it sail over the car into the median. As I felt the car lift in the air to roll over, I screamed," Jesus!"

Suddenly the car skidded to an abrupt halt and settled across the highway, blocking the entire path for the vehicles heading around the curve toward me. The car had quit, but started quickly, and it was somehow able to drag the trailer and boat into the median inches before the traffic crashed into me. There is no explanation how a car can drag a huge boat with a wheel missing and an axle that, we learned later, had cracked completely in half!

Jesus brought me an answer to every request I made in most amazing ways! He brought me a trucker who disconnected my car. I went to a phone to call my husband,

and a Christian man in the store offered to weld my broken hitch and repair it. I was required to place warning triangles around the boat and trailer. I could not find any for the amount of cash I had, and they didn't yet accept credit cards. A thought came, after praying, to walk around a corner. A sign in the window announced the triangles were on sale for EXACTLY the amount I had, $19. God surrounded me with peace. I knew I was not in control.

I called my husband, who had to pick up a new axle in South Georgia. The only company who carries this unusual axle had none left, but was making one right then. It would be finished by the time he got there. So Roger took off at 2AM in a borrowed truck whose owner failed to give him a gas cap key.

He arrived in Cleveland in time to have breakfast with me. We then went to the highway to check out the boat trailer. It had disappeared! We searched everywhere, and could not find it. It was not transportable with a cracked axle and no tire. We were astounded and confused.

Again we called on the Lord, and found a policeman in town to file a report for a stolen trailer and boat. A woman walking past overheard us, of all things, and said she had seen one being towed by a wrecker up the highway at 8PM the evening before. She even knew the name of the wrecking company in the next town!

We found it right where she had said to go. What a blessing to pay a fair towing fee, and to have a safe place to repair the trailer. The owner of the lot even loaned us his tools.

I was the go-fer, so I hunted two tires, a bearing race and other things. The tires were a unique size, and nobody had them in three towns. The last place I stopped was a junkyard, and after learning they had none, I sat on some tires to call other towns. I asked the Lord what to do, and the clerk yelled out a "Wow! Can you believe this?" I said," What?" He said, "Lady, you are sitting on the very tires you need!" He sold them to me for $10! (It was 1979.)

I found the race and other things at a store ten miles or so from where my husband was working to tear down the trailer. When I returned to him, the race was missing from the bag. I found they had also forgotten to charge me for it. But Roger examined the wheel and realized he hadn't needed one after all. God knew it all the time. He was 'way ahead of me.

Soon the new axle was in place, and Roger and our son Rob drove the car and trailer. I followed in the van. He had not been able to repair the trailer brakes, however, so I was rather nervous about having him drive through the mountains to get home. I followed, praying in the spirit the entire time.

We got to a steep mountain with a curve in it, of course, and I noticed the car had begun to sway a great deal. Suddenly I realized the nightmare had returned! They were headed for a steel rail, beyond which was a huge area of nothing! I screamed for Jesus again, and miraculously, just as before, they straightened out! They kept going as if nothing had happened, and I stopped at a rest area that was at the next turn, and cried. I was exhausted from lack of sleep, and so relieved that they were all right. I just had to stop.

After calming down, I turned the key, and the van would not start! Within a half an hour, the entire population of the rest area was surrounding me, trying to help. Nothing worked. Then my brain kicked into gear, and I remembered what the Lord had done! I sat down in the midst of the group and prayed that the Lord would start the van. I got in, turned the key, and took off! Praise God! They just stood there staring at me. I should have started preaching!

The next event God used to show me He hears me was that I noticed my gas was nearly gone. I told the Lord my problem...I had no cash and no gas cap key! A thought came to follow a semi-truck ahead of me. I followed him off an exit, and soon saw a gas station. I explained to the attendant my situation, and he reached in his pocket for a key, and opened my gas cap with it! He also took MasterCard.

This was only a few of the many miracles God did on this trip. Whenever I am tempted to get discouraged, I remember what God has done for me in the past. The list is so very, very long!

How does God give what we need? He has a still small voice, which speaks within our mind. Call it a thought; call it the mind of Christ. I believe God can do it any way He wants.

HANDS OFF MY OUIJA BOARD
By Beth Plagenhof

We know that there are two sources of spiritual influence in the world today, God and Satan. Let me tell you how I was fooled and taken in by Satan. It took an act of God to open my eyes to the wrong I had been doing.

A few years ago I became interested in psychic phenomenon. I joined a book club, which would supply me with all the information I wanted concerning spiritualists, mind reading, astrology, clairvoyance, psychometry*, ESP, dreams, and meditation. For the record, I am not a 'way out' type person. I have been a born-again Christian for fifteen years, graduated from a large University, and now am an average housewife with young children. We are active members of a Dutch Reformed Church.

I began to read everything I could find about psychic phenomena. I did not think I was turning away from God. I wanted to be close to God and let His Spirit work in and through me. All of my Christian life I had felt dissatisfied and did not feel that I had the power of God in my life. So I studied and read and my precious book collection grew and grew.

I took further action and bought a Ouija board. A friend and I decided to have some fun. To our amazement, our questions were answered. The planchette flew under our fingers. We felt the power which we knew was not ours. We began to ask serious questions and an 'angel' was our guide. He could give beautiful sermons and quote scripture. He *claimed he could provide us with 'deeper' truths than the Bible.* He said we could communicate with anyone in heaven. Dead relatives were impersonated with great skill.

Soon I was doing automatic writing. It was much faster than the board. The writing would not be in my own handwriting. I relaxed my hand and the spirit simply took over. Usually my whole arm would go numb. The pencil would travel at great speed. Ruth Montgomery, who writes about Jean Dixon, uses automatic writing on her typewriter. Mrs. Montgomery believes she communicates with her departed father.

After a while the messages came into my mind. The spirits were very helpful. They would tell me the time even before I opened my eyes in the morning. They told me where things were when I lost them. (Satan counterfeits God's gifts, so God can also do these things. Satan is an 'angel of light', to deceive us.) The spirits predicted the outcome of things in the future. I was happy. I had ESP.

The next summer I visited a Spiritualist camp. After a meeting the minister and a lady demonstrated their psychic powers. People in the audience agreed as to the findings and dead relatives had properly made their appearances. The minister looked at me and said, "Why aren't you up here? Don't you know you have these powers?" I said I didn't think so, and no thank you. I was just a visitor. Actually I was frightened of the whole atmosphere and could not wait to leave.

The spirits started telling me that God wanted me to be a medium. This could be my way of helping people. They tried to put me in a trance. I would feel very heavy, and sleepy spells made me go unconscious. But for some reason I didn't understand then, I never made it. Thank God!

With two friends, I visited a sweet lady who has strong psychic ability. She gave each of us a reading, using her gift of psychometry. She would hold our ring or watch and see in her head signs and symbols which would tell her about the owner of the article she held. She was very accurate in her predictions, but she thanked Jesus for her gifts. She should have thanked Satan.

I started practicing psychometry. Thoughts and feelings did start to come. I did not know that this was Satan's counterfeit for God's gifts of wisdom and knowledge. Close relatives and friends were concerned for me and asked me to stop all my nonsense. But I would not listen to anyone.

I tried to find a medium to talk to, not to get in on a séance, for I could contact my own spirits, but simply to get advice and further knowledge. For some mysterious reason, doors always shut in my face when I tried. On a trip in California I called two mediums, and one hung up on me and the other was never home. God had His hand on me, and was only permitting me to go so far.

That summer I met a Holy Spirit filled woman. She was concerned and prayed for me. I had learned of the Baptism in the Holy Spirit and was seeking it, although in subtle ways the evil spirits were trying to keep me away from Spirit-filled people and once did keep me from visiting a Pentecostal Church in another city.

God, however, was working, and He was starting to bring me back to Him. Doubts crept in concerning my 'psychic powers'. I turned to God in prayer. I prayed for Jesus to forgive me all my sins and to bring to my attention sins I had committed unknowingly. I asked Jesus to fill me with His Holy Spirit. He did! Jesus was with me that night in a very real way. I wept with joy. I praised my Lord in an unknown language for a long time. I had been a lost sheep and gone astray, but God had cared for me and brought me home.

The next night after prayer, I could not sleep. God was trying to tell me something. I prayed more and thought about my Ouija board. "You don't need it any more," God was trying to tell me. For two hours, I was wrestling with these thoughts. Finally I said, "Okay, Jesus, tomorrow I'll get rid of it." I can do automatic writing, so the board is archaic anyway." Sleep still would not come. Then the word, "Obey" went through my mind and I knew it was not my thought. So at five AM I got up and destroyed my Ouija board. Sleep came immediately after that. Talking with my friend the next day we were amazed that

God had dealt with us on the same night on the same subject, and both of us had destroyed our boards.

The second thing God wanted me to do was to get rid of my book collection. I obeyed, and about $200 worth of books went up in smoke.

I went to a prayer meeting the same week, and the woman who had been praying for me handed me some material and a letter to read. The material was against witchcraft, astrology, hypnotists, and automatic writing. But it didn't convince me. I still did not think that automatic writing was evil. But one line in the letter stood out. The verse in the Bible I had used to test the spirits was not a valid test for Satan. I was horrified. I picked up a pencil and asked my 'angel' if he loved Christ. Yes, he did. Did he love Satan? Yes, he did. He revealed himself to me as he really was – a demon. He had impersonated all the other spirits. He laughed at me and said he hated me. I went into prayer and begged God's forgiveness, and I thanked God for opening my eyes.

A minister gave me the book, "The Challenging Counterfeit" by Raphael Gasson. I learned that Satan has counterfeits for the true gifts of the Holy Spirit. But those who are filled with the greater power of the Holy Spirit can defeat Satan's power.

It makes me sad that Satan is doing the same good works which the Lord commissioned His disciples to do, while the church with all the supernatural powers of God at its disposal is neglecting to seek after the gifts. I pray that God's children will wake up and learn not to inquire into these things of Satan's counterfeits. It will only lead you further away from God, not nearer as I believed. If you have any spirit in your life that you can use, then it is NOT the Holy Spirit.

You can't use God. Most people don't have the least idea of the reality of demons. So many people believed me when I said I thought my powers were from God. And why not believe that Jean Dixon's powers are God-given? They say, "Look at all the good work she does. And she says herself she believes in God and prays every day." I now realize that evil spirits work for her. She and her followers are being greatly deceived.

The areas of witchcraft, sorcery, horoscopes, black magic, astrology, Yoga, oriental cults, hypnotism, Ouija boards, automatic writing, Spiritism and the rest are all Satan's territory. I wish to have nothing to do with him or his false gifts.

Jesus has set me free. I am so grateful that He loved me enough to bring me back to Him. My life is now committed fully to Jesus Christ. I stand on the Word of God, the precious Holy Bible.

I pray that people who are involved in any of Satan's areas will turn away from it and call on God's Spirit for help. The Bible says in James 4:7-8, "Submit yourselves therefore to God. Resist the devil, and he will flee from you. Draw near to God, and He will draw near to you."

I pray that those good people who poke fun at these things and say these are only games, I say to you, please wake up! One of Satan's cleverest tricks is to convince people that he doesn't exist.

Demons are real, and they do have supernatural power. Don't underestimate them.

Turn to God and seek His gifts. Don't settle for Satan's counterfeits. I cannot thank God enough for bringing me back to Him and opening my eyes to the truth!

*Psychometry is defined as the divination of facts concerning an object or its owner through contact with or proximity to the object.

Beth adds:

When I was in the occult, God never left me. He still loved me and He called me back to Him. My repentance came in a flood of tears for having grieved God so much. I had many invitations to speak concerning my involvement, but my husband at that time was against it.

I cringe when I hear Christians talk about their 'horoscope' or having a 'ghost in the house, or get trapped into believing some New Age idea. We need to be grounded in the Word of God, not a TV program, not a trend (like angels), nor holistic methods that are a counterfeit of God's ways.

My deception was so strong that I wouldn't listen to people telling me I was wrong. It bothered me deeply that a spirit-filled woman was concerned about me and was praying for me. I thought, "There is nothing wrong with me." But God answered her prayers and it was through His power that I was set free.

Then God tested me. After I was set free, I was sitting at the kitchen table one day making out a grocery list. I relaxed my pen over the paper, thinking about what food I needed. Then the pen started writing, "Call me." I was shocked! I dropped it as if it was on fire! I rebuked it, and sent it away in Jesus' name. Then I prayed. Later, I thanked God, because it hit me. The demon had no more power over me. He needed my permission, my invitation, in order to enter my life again. This time, and for eternity, he doesn't have it. Jesus set me free, and I am free indeed!

Inspiration

Listen to my voice and obey it in the little mundane things you must accomplish daily. Discipline does not begin with the largest weakness you have. It begins with minor ones. As they are conquered, you gain strength for greater challenges.

You have won. Claim the treasure. Self-control is indeed, as you have recalled, the fruit of the Spirit. Have all these fruits ripened at once? No, the roots are still growing. They will continue to grow. Do you know how the roots of a vine grow? They grow beneath the surface in a longitudinal direction. Many new plants branch from them as they will from you as your roots strengthen. Does the vine plan to do this? No, it is made this way. My power does this.

You will draw others to you. You will not need to put forth an effort. When comfort is needed, they will be reminded of your concern for them, and they will seek you out. Just be there. I will give you the words of comfort when they are prepared for them. My Spirit does not use force. You must not use coercion, trickery, or any of the world's ways to bring men to me. None come to me but by the Spirit of God. They have no understanding of spiritual things lest I reveal them.

Your duty is obedience. I will lead you into sharing in my time. Have you decided you will be an evangelist? This is my decision. Watch for signs which will show you my tasks for you. You will soon be ready to bring forth fruits of my labor."

On Fire!

Exposure to demons comes in many forms. My Christian nurse friend Betty screamed my name on the phone, "Help me! I'm on fire!"

I didn't understand what she was talking about. I yelled into the phone, "Hang up! Get out! I will call the fire department!"

She frantically got through to me that the fire was in her body. I ran to my car, rushed the four miles to her apartment, and burst through the unlocked door. Curled up on the center of her bed covered with vomit, wide-eyed and hysterical, lay my dear Christian friend. She was cold as ice to the touch.

Jesus had to teach me what to pray. Words floated in my brain, "Cast out the spirit of fear." I took the authority He speaks of in Matthew 18:19, and those few simple words and His powerful name set her free! Too simple? Betty was instantly relieved of a tormenting devil that had taken residence in her body. Can Christians be tormented by demons? They can if they go where God forbids them. Her spirit was not affected but her body was.

Weeping with relief, she got cleaned up, and shared her story. She had drifted away from church, her support system, after her husband divorced her, and the Mormons began wooing her. They found her an apartment next to them- one family on each side of her. They brought her to dinner, gave her food and met her needs like Christians would have done. She got confused; their doctrines sounded so Christ-like.

She did not realize how crucial it was to remain with true believers, that life involves a battle in the mind. She had nobody to bounce off her thoughts. Two believers can literally turn away ten thousand evil spirits, and a 'triple-braided cord' is not easily broken. Eccles. 4:12.

I had come to check on her one day after her move and this 'firestorm.' The Mormon neighbors appeared at her door and busted right in without knocking, surrounding me, with smiles pasted on their mouth but with their eyes glaring at me. Every time I tried to talk about Jesus, they began quoting the Mormon Bible to her. I saw her confusion, and realized I was not getting through.

Friends prayed with me for her release, and she soon stopped going to the Mormon church. They began to threaten her. "We have given you our very lives. We helped you find a home. How can you do this to us? You may find yourself having an accident. I would be very careful if I were you." She got really scared and soon moved away.

After that one deliverance, she has been victorious ever since. She stays close to true

Christians at all times, and is doing very well.

Some experts explain Mormonism is not Christianity. Apparently there are serious semantics involved. In truth, Jesus was on the cross while God the Father was not. God turned His back on His Son for a moment because all the sin of the world was upon Him for our sake.   God is three distinct beings- Father, Son and Holy Ghost, three in one- a Trinity. But clearly scripture also says Jesus is God. "*If you have seen Me, you have seen the Father,*" Jesus said. Many other scriptures reveal the same truth. We are not meant to understand it all; it is by faith. I hope one day all the half-truths various religions have will dissipate and we can all be one big family! We are to love all people, even our enemies. Bottom line.

Is the Baptism in the Holy Ghost a command or an option?

God says there are those with a form of religion but lack the power. Who will survive persecution if it comes and which will more likely fall away? To ask for the Holy Spirit is definitely a command. We can disobey it, but we miss out on great gifts.

Now the church was filled with power. From that moment, miracles were the norm for the church. Signs and wonders followed those that believed. Thousands were added to the church. They drove the "religious" people nuts- just like we do today.

I was thrilled in 1974 to have been baptized in the Holy Spirit. I was in bed praying, and asked the Lord Jesus to fill me with His Spirit. Suddenly I was pressed against the bed with a weakness that was difficult to explain. I knew I could have resisted and it would have lifted, but I also knew if I did not surrender to Him, He would not have given me what I asked for.

My heart began pounding in a new way with a great Boom Boom Boom, and I could feel what I cannot describe in human terms. Love is not tangible, but all I can say is that LOVE began to permeate every cell. Every part of me was filling with an ecstasy I have never experienced and I knew I was dying from the awesome magnificent power coming into me. And I didn't care. There was no fear in that dying experience, but a oneness with the creator that I still am unable to explain. Words formed in my head and were forming in my mouth, but I stifled them from coming out, because my husband was asleep next to me. God is a gentleman and does not force us to do anything. I knew it was a language that God was trying to give me. After a few minutes, I simply fell asleep.

The next day, I was beside myself with joy, that unspeakable joy God talks about. I went to the dentist that day, and in the waiting room, I shared with a sweet Christian woman what had happened. She carefully responded with a statement that shook my faith almost to the point of shattering me! She was a pastor's mother, and I trusted her credentials. She said, "Sweetheart, you had an experience that was an attempt of Satan to deceive you. God doesn't do this in our day any more. The people in the Bible needed to know other languages to preach to all those from other countries. Now we have interpreters to do that. I am so sorry. Just repent and tell God you are sorry for seeking supernatural signs. He will forgive you."

I was devastated! I believed her completely. I was a year old Christian and had a teachable spirit, but this really terrified me, to think I could be so deceived. I even went to my pastor, and he reinforced what she had said, showing me verses about 'tongues will pass away', and that we are baptized in the Holy Spirit when born again and that is the baptism Jesus told us would happen to believers. (But He tells us to ask.) He showed me the verse that said there is only one baptism. (actually there are more – yes, there is one baptism into the body of Christ, Jesus' water baptism with John, God sending the spirit down to Jesus like a dove, water baptism for the church, a baptism of suffering, baptism of fire, and baptism of the Holy Ghost for believers if they ask Jesus.

Thank God for those that walk beside new believers and disciple them. God gave me one of the few in our church that understood the truth. She went through the word and explained what it really said, and not out of context. She put my feet on a solid foundation again. After all this, I woke the next night to find my room filled with a supernatural light! It remained in the room about ten minutes, and nothing could be seen but that peaceful light. I was wide awake. Rog slept through it all. I was awestruck over this presence in the room. No words were spoken, nobody appeared, but God was there. It left slowly and the room was again dark.

My former church preached about miracles, but when they did not manifest except very rarely, people stopped expecting them. They had to assume miracles, signs and wonders were not for today. They were just stories from Bible times.

I am certain many preachers have prayed for the Holy Spirit baptism, just to experiment and see if it is really true as we say. But if taught against it, their doubts stand in the way of receiving. James says a double-minded (doubting) man receives nothing from the Lord.

My friend asked Jesus to baptize her with the Holy Ghost. She felt nothing and noticed nothing. But over the next three weeks, memories came to the surface, making her weep over her sins and those done to her. After the three weeks, a sudden joy filled her, and a new language poured from her mouth as she worshiped God.

We live in a world of logic- a rational world. The Spirit of God begins to woo us and seek after us. God gives every man a measure of faith. If we respond and receive what He offers, He comes into us. We are now members of a different kingdom, with a different ruler than before. We are free of Satan's rule over us.

We have entered a new realm. We are not of this world. We are aliens in a foreign land. We have been invited to participate with the Holy Spirit to spread this message to others. What an honor! Jesus came to destroy the works of the devil. We are given power to do the same thing. The nine fruits of the Spirit pour into us as God moves in us. The supernatural gifts manifest as God does His work in response to our faith. The work God asks of us is to believe. I must add that I believe this experience gives us extra power but we are certainly going to heaven without it. It does not alter our salvation.

Mark 16:17 *And these signs will accompany those who believe; in my name they will drive out demons. They will speak in new tongues; 18 they will pick up snakes with their hands; and when they drink deadly poison, it will not hurt them at all; they will place their hands on sick people and they will get well.*

Here are a few articles about belief systems we need to understand.

Postmodernism

"But of the fruit of the tree which *is* in the midst of the garden, God hath said, Ye shall not eat of it, neither shall ye touch it, lest ye die." Genesis 3:3 This was the tree of the knowledge of good and evil. Adam and Eve were allowed to eat of the tree of life. They chose wrongly. That wrong choice still brings mankind into hopelessness.

This belief system goes beyond the old 'modernism' where reason was the worldview, truth was relative, open to everything, tolerant of everyone's beliefs, man subjugates (conquers, subdues) the earth and males dominate. It is without hope of anything deep or eternal.

Postmodernism surpasses modernism, rejects the authority of reason, believes objective truth is dangerous, that it is arrogant, evil, and intolerant to point out errors of another's religious beliefs, and personal choice is the basis for spiritual truth. Missionaries are judgmental and unnecessary, if not dangerous. Fundamentalists are people subject to rational investigation. Reason and truth is political and subversive. Man is to accept all beliefs as valid. No one can really be lost.

GeoBarna.com's research says 4 out of 10 adults believe most religions pray to the same God. Less than half born again Christians agree reaching the lost is important. They have absorbed the worldviews around them. Christians now divorce and abort babies at the same rate as the world, revealing their exposure to non-Christian views.

People with this view are led by feelings, and are not responsible or accountable to anyone. Their morality is based on choice alone. They discern nothing.

This, for Christians, covers it. Ecclesiastes 12: 13-*14 Let us hear the conclusion of the whole matter: Fear God, and keep his commandments: for this is the whole duty of man. [14] For God shall bring every work into judgment, with every secret thing, whether it be good, or whether it be evil.*

How can we reach people with what we know to be truth? They have set up barriers against every effort. Pray the Holy Spirit draws them and pulls down the strongholds in their minds- mind-blinding spirits. Build a relationship, live for Christ, ask good questions, tell your own story, encourage them to read the Bible in an easy version, guide them to John, help them talk about who Jesus is.

They need to know they are precious to God, their Creator, and that He purchased them with His redeeming blood. Ask them their purpose in life, and show God has a purpose for them. I Cor. 5:11-15 and Ephesians 1:4-5 helps. God said His word will not return void, but will accomplish that for which it was sent.

Knowing truth is possible, not based on feelings, but facts and faith. Wonderful feelings follow. (The joy of the Lord is our strength.)

Help them examine the evidence that truth exists. Does the world reflect a Creator? Does history reveal God's intervention? Is there evidence He seeks to communicate with man? Plant seeds. Others will water them. God will reveal Himself. We simply do our part.

Kingdom of the Cults

My father-in-law introduced his sons to Demolay, an organization for teens related to the Freemasons. Rog became a diligent student and worked up the ranks, in later years becoming a Master Mason, and held the rank of *Worshipful Master*. He gave his life to this organization, having made vows that would stand your hair on end IF you took them seriously. But it is "all in fun". Right? Wrong. God listened. The vows were made with a hand on the Bible with an oath to the Great Architect, which can only be God Almighty.

Later in his life, he got involved with church. The consistory found out he was a Mason, and warned him about its evils. He couldn't hear or understand what in the world they were talking about. "Surely they simply do not understand this is a wonderful organization, with love and brotherhood for all. They are all deluded." He was hurt over their rejection and left the church. He did not return for over twenty years.

Those that have gone beyond the first 32 studies or degrees know more about it, but they did not reveal the meaning of the rituals to him.   To him, they simply symbolized King Solomon and his temple.

Rog, a dear man, was unwittingly worshipping a false god. God said, "You shall have no other gods before Me. For I, the Lord, am a jealous God, visiting the iniquity of the fathers on the children, to the third and fourth generation of those who hate Me." There is one true God. Freemasons claim Allah, Buddha, God, and every other deity as worthy of honor, by inviting all faiths to join with them in their rituals. They bow to a man; they call a man 'Worshipful'. Only God is worthy of such honor.

So if God visits the sins of our ancestors upon us, how are they manifested? Do we perhaps attribute a spirit of infirmity to such curses? Rheumatoid arthritis? Diabetes? Deafness? Hydrocephaly? Dementia?

How does God "visit iniquity?" Jesus was pierced for our iniquities (sins). Does this mean once we are saved, these curses will have no effect on us once we are believers? "No curse can alight without a cause." This is the big question. We need to find the answer to this important question.

His brother also followed his father into Freemasonry. He was the youngest man in Michigan to have a heart attack of this type, at 27 years old. The man was plagued with one illness after another, having had open-heart surgery twice and in need of another when he died. It began when he became a Mason. His daughter married, and finds she is barren. There is no explanation.

When we married, my father-in-law was a Freemason as I said. My mother-in-law was in the Eastern Star. For twenty years our activities centered on Masonry and the Shrine. There was a lot of drinking and partying in the Shrine, but not so much with the Masons.

Roger renounced Masonry a few years ago when he was afraid of dying from a heart problem he had. He had fallen down the stairs and nearly blew out his heart valve! Friends shared an audiotape with him the night before surgery and he realized he had been deceived, having considered Freemasonry simply a brotherhood organization. He sensed his physical problems might have connections with his mistaken devotion to the wrong god. He repented of his involvement and renounced Masonry that night.

The next day he had open heart surgery with two bypasses and a new valve, and had absolutely no pain during several weeks of recovery, which was a great miracle. Others in the waiting rooms with him had no such a blessing after their similar surgery!

Our friend Bob spent many years in Mormonism. When he learned the deception in Mormonism and the ties to Masonry, (the founder of Mormonism, Joseph Smith and his brother Hyrum, were also Masons.) Bob began to study over a thousand books on both religions (yes, Masonry IS a religion), including cryptic books for Masons only. He now speaks all over the country, mostly in churches. One day he went to a funeral and the hair on his neck stood up. He turned to see a group of men marching in with aprons on, wearing white gloves, chanting and breaking leaves over the coffin. His Masonic father said he wanted a funeral like that. "Over my dead body!" our friend said. His father later renounced Masonry and died a Christian, devoted only to Jesus Christ.

The following information came from an article called, "Freemasonry and the Church" by Ed Decker. (Type in 'Christians and Freemasonry.') Used with permission.

Masonry began benignly with the stonemasons in Solomon's time. They learned secret handshakes and signs to show other masons they belonged to the craft of stonemasonry, but nothing more. Spiritual Masonry began much later. The first Grand lodge met in England in 1717. Masonry was involved in the French and American Revolutions, and a conspiratorial part of

America's history. Many in the first
Congress were Masons. The Declaration of
Independence was written on a Masonic
white lambskin apron. Masons designed the
Congressional Medal of Honor, which has
on it a pentagram, the most powerful satanic
emblem.

The statue of Liberty was a gift from
Masons in France to the American Masons.
It is filled with occult symbols.

Initiates are told this is a brotherhood
organization that allows all religions to join,
and that it is not a religion, but it definitely
is. It is not Christian, by any means. The
secret identity of God is Jabulon, and stands
for Jehovah, Ba'al, and Osiris, the Egyptian
sun god. The swearing-in ceremony and the
rituals make this a religion in honor of
demons. The key demon is the Goat of
Mendes or Baphomet.

When a Mason receives his apron, he is told
it should be his covering when they stand
before the great white throne judgment of
God. They don't realize this is the judgment
of the damned!

The 'sacred' word learned at a certain level of the Scottish rite is Abbadon. This is the angel of the bottomless pit. Rev.9:11

Blue Lodge members are sworn to keep brethren's secrets, murder and treason excepted. Royal Arch Masons are sworn to protect even murder and treason. Imagine going to a court of law and expecting a fair trial when the judge is upholding first his oath to the Masons. If you hear of a crazy court case that is not going fairly, you might examine the roots of Masonry.

Scriptures and Bible teachings are sometimes quoted in Masonry but the name of Jesus Christ is generally omitted.

Those that partake of only the first thirty-two degrees of Masonry, though they have made terrible vows, have not taken communion of the dead, drinking wine from a human skull, as in the higher levels of the Scottish rite, I believe it was the 33rd degree.

Once they study and pass the 32nd degree, they may go into the Shrine-for a price, of course. Their vows include an oath that says,

"May Allah, the god of Arab, Moslem, and Mohammedan, the god of our fathers, support me…" Allah is not God the Father of Jesus Christ! It is a deity entombed in a building in Mecca where Islam worships it. No Christian can submit to or swear allegiance to this other god, Allah.

Why is the Fez they wear red? The Muslims butchered forty-five thousand people in the city of Fez that refused to bow to Allah. They dipped their white hats in the blood of the Christian martyrs.

The Orlando Sentinel published a report about the percentage of the money collected by Shriners went to the Shrine hospitals. You may check for yourself.

If families of Masons are having sickness or any other cursed things bothering them, they need to examine their relationship with God. He is a jealous God, and has a right to be. He gave His only Son to save us. Nobody else deserves our allegiance. Masonry brings a curse into families to the third and fourth generation of those that have turned from God. God honors repentance from the heart and forgives sin.

Only Freemasons can become Shriners.

There are many Masons sitting in churches unaware that they have been disloyal to God. They simply have been deceived. It does not help to condemn them, but pray and share what you know to be true if they will listen. Many great articles are found on the Internet.

Freedom!

Stories are woven through this book as evidence that deliverance is important, but first let's lay a foundation.

What is it like to be reborn? When we realize that Jesus is really part of God and lived on earth, was murdered and rose again three days later, we have received a profound revelation! Once we understand that as sinners we have no right to be forgiven by God or enter heaven when we die, we seek further. We learn that God sent Jesus to die in our place.

He was what the Old Testament called a perfect Lamb. God's law stated that a lamb without blemish must be given to the priest as payment for sins one had committed. That was only temporary and had to be repeated from time to time. Jesus' blood was a permanent sacrifice. If we accept Him as our Lamb and confess to God that He paid for us, God forgives all our sins. He sends His spirit to live inside us and change us over time into His image.

Self must be dealt with and allowed to "die" with Christ, and Christ must be allowed to reign in the person's heart and mind. Once we learn what it means to be dead to sin and alive to God we begin to live an overcoming life. Focusing on ourselves rather than on Jesus in us makes us self-conscious and reminds us of our old sin nature. Then we often try to overcome sin with will power as Satan begins to toy with us. We in our strength cannot overcome him, and we must trust Jesus to do it in us.

As we search the Word of God for guidance and peace, joy gives us the strength we need to get through life. Self, or flesh, becomes our idol in a way if we depend on our own strength to be what we know God calls us to be. It is not about us at all. It is all about Jesus in us. Like John said, "I must decrease and He must increase." We cannot be perfect or even decent by willpower alone.

Once we are totally convinced of the truth in the scriptures for our own lives, we are assured of God's unconditional love for us. We are unable, unable to disappoint Jesus! It is impossible! And when the Father looks down on us, He sees us through the blood of

Christ, with all sin washed away. He sees us as righteous as Jesus. That is hard to believe but that is what faith is all about. Faith and God's grace saves us.

What is grace? It is His favor. You and I are His very favorites…just because we didn't reject Jesus or His plan to save us by His own power. It is not about us. Once we understand this, we are free to just be, and let God develop us into His image over time. He said we will know the truth and the truth will set us free. This is the truth.

Some of us desire ecstatic feelings from time to time in our walk with God. Do the lost people 'feel' lost? Then why must we 'feel' saved? It is a temptation to seek the goosebumps when the real 'feelings' that God gives are those of peace and serenity, knowing all is well with our soul. We can get into trouble seeking feelings instead of seeking a close relationship with God instead. This again is our flesh looking for satisfaction, not our spirit man. Feelings do not prove our spirituality, and again move our focus to that old man, self, which rears its ugly head trying to be resurrected. We are told to reckon ourselves dead to sin and alive to Christ, putting Him first in our lives by faith in His forgiveness and His love for us.

Jesus said in John 12:25 *"He who loves his life will lose it, and he who hates his life in this world shall keep it to life eternal."* It is saying we live an exchanged life. We trade ours for His. I hope that makes sense to you. Study the words hate and lose.

What freedom there is when we can be transparent and free from needing to please anyone, not even ourselves. We trust God and it does not matter to us what anyone says about us or to us, or what they think. Only God matters. We automatically please other believers walking the same way without even trying, because God's love is free to pour through us to them. It is the way of life, and it is wonderful.

Power from the Holy Spirit

What does God say about the Holy Spirit? There are many views, some even coming from seminaries, but only what God says is the truth. When something happens to you, nobody can take that away from you. If a spiritual experience does not line up with the Bible, however, it is not from God, and is best set aside. If it does, you have God's Word backing up your experience, and it gives validity to it.

The disciples were witnesses to the existence and power of the Holy Spirit of God, the third person of the Trinity. I am also a witness of this because the same thing happened to me!

It was 1974. I had become a believer in Jesus Christ and salvation, and had hungrily studied the Bible. It was a wonderful time in my life, because suddenly I could now understand what I was reading! The Bible is not like other books. It is written in such a way that unless God is helping you, it makes little sense. Remember the funny 3-D glasses we wore years ago to see three-dimensional movies? You could see a little without them, but not much. All of a sudden, the picture came into focus with the glasses! This is what it is like to invite Jesus into your life. He empowers us to understand spiritual things.

In Luke 3:16, John tells of one greater than he, who will baptize with the Holy Ghost and with fire. Jesus is the baptizer, and it means immersion.

I studied in my concordance every verse about the words: Holy Ghost, Holy Spirit, baptisms (there are seven), power, and gifts. I got a good overview of the Spirit's functions in our lives and knew I needed the Lord Jesus to do this for me.

My husband was asleep in bed next to me, and I whispered, "Jesus, will you please baptize me in the Holy Spirit?" Instantly He responded! I began feeling wonderfully different! My heart began beating with an unusual rhythm, and I can only explain it as feeling like God poured liquid love into every cell of my being! I have no earthly words to describe the ecstasy. Strange words formed in my mind, but I refused to open my mouth, not wanting to wake my husband. I was beside myself with "joy unspeakable and full of glory", as the disciples said. Jesus offered me a special gift of a new language with which to praise Him, but I held it inside.

Five months later, I was singing with the radio while driving, and found myself singing in a language I had not learned! God can do whatever He wants. We just let Him know we trust Him, and expect it. He is full of surprises! I learned that any time I wish to pray in my new language, I simply decide and am able to. He needs my vocal cords, however.

Why do I love this gift? Ephesians six says praying in the Spirit is part of our spiritual armor. It says to pray in the Spirit at all times. I generally pray this way alone because it says it is better when praying publicly that others know what we are saying or they cannot agree.

When I am too distraught to know what to pray about, the Holy Spirit knows all things and intercedes for me in ways I do not even know about. The problem dissolves and I know the prayer has taken care of it. Great peace overtakes me during these times.

One time, six friends were praying for my friend Virginia, who was scheduled to have a breast lump removed. She was quite afraid. Her husband, still an unbeliever, agreed to pray with us. We stood in a circle holding hands, and prayed as we felt led. I distinctly sensed that God was speaking within me, telling me to pray aloud in my new language. I was very self-conscious, as this was a very precious and personal thing for me. But I began to pray in whatever language God gave me.

Virginia's husband quickly let go my hand as if it was on fire! He yelled," What are you doing?" I got real nervous and explained that I was praying in my prayer language. He asked what I was saying, and I said I didn't know. (The Bible says one is not to speak in tongues in public unless an interpreter is present, so I felt I was out of order.) Ken said he was able to interpret every word, because it was pure Latin, and he had taken four years of Latin in college! This dear man was convicted of his need to be a Christian as a result of what the Holy Spirit spoke through me-in Latin!

Ken was wonderfully saved that day, and we all rejoiced with him. Strangely enough, a year later, this man unexpectedly died. Just think how God used this gift to save him. By the way – God also healed Virginia without the need of surgery!

Some have received this gift when others put their hands on their heads and prayed. Others just wait after asking, and it happens shortly. In Acts 2, Jesus' followers waited many days in an upper room. When they 'were all in one accord' one hundred twenty were present. The Lord sent the Holy Spirit into the room 'like a mighty wind'. Tongues of what looked like fire rested on each of them, and each spoke in other tongues 'as the Spirit gave utterance.'

Shortly after my experience, I was sharing with a Christian lady about it. She said something that greatly confused me by telling me in a kind way that I had been deceived by the devil and it had come from him! I went home in emotional shock! She was a mother of a pastor. But after studying the Bible, I realized she was mistaken, and God had given me a precious gift, just as He promised.

Fear Has Torment

There is no fear in love; but perfect love casteth out fear: because fear hath torment. He that feareth is not made perfect in love. I John 4:18 For God hath not given us the spirit of fear; but of power, and of love, and of a sound mind. 2 Timothy 1:7

Howard Hughes had so much money he didn't know what to do with it, but he could not buy his way out of fear. The poor man died like an animal, in terrible torment. He had a phobia about germs that imprisoned him. He didn't know Jesus had dominion over his fears and would have gladly set him free if he would give his life to Him.

How do people cope with fear on a daily basis? Where fear resides paralysis occurs. We are frozen to inaction. It is hard to act when one is gripped by fear. Courage is acting even though fear is surrounding you. Without courage, we would surely die a slow and painful death via fear, one action or inaction at a time. Matthew 28:4 *And the guards shook for fear of him, and became like dead men.* Why should we hand over our lives to fear and sit paralyzed at its mercy?

Satan desires to bring us fear of giving our testimony. Once he has messed with our intimacy with Christ, he sets out to shut us down, making us ineffective for God. Silencing our testimony and ministry for Christ is the greatest gift Satan can hope for at this point. Fear helps him obtain that goal.

There is such a thing as a spirit called 'fear', and it is terrifying. How do we counteract such a power? The name of Jesus has this power. Certain words in the Bible are just like swords against spirit beings we cannot even see. Demons bow to the name of Jesus.

I thought of a dear friend of mine. The other night we were having a good conversation about God and His promises, and how trustworthy He is. Suddenly the conversation took a dramatic shift, and she began talking about demon experiences. Some ill wind blew in that could be felt! It was shocking. We went from peace to a feeling of panic in less than a minute! It hit her and flowed right into me!

An actual entity either entered the room by invitation of some sort, or it was my vivid imagination. I am convinced there is such a thing as a spirit called 'fear', and it is a terrifying thing. How do we counteract such a power? The name of Jesus has such power. Certain words in the Bible are just like swords against spirit beings we cannot even see.

□ □ □

Sometimes evil spirits live in people. One such time was when a very crude woman came to my house to pick up a car our son Tom had repaired. She was determined to drive it off without paying, and Tom was not a fighter. He was going to let her take it. In righteous indignation, my blood started to boil. "You may have your car when you pay Tom for the hard work he has done for you." I demanded she pay or leave my property. A fear came at me that made my body jerk like an electric shock hit it. It took all of God's Spirit in me to withstand it! My knees were knocking together and my heart was pounding fast; the spirit was attacking my body.

I was thankful my car was parked behind hers. She stomped down my driveway and left, swearing at us both. But an hour later, she returned and threw the money to the ground at Tom's feet. I picked it up while he cautiously handed her the key to her car. I barely got my car out of the way before she swerved around it and skidded away.

☐ ☐ ☐

Another time my knees shook was when my husband introduced me to Janet, a woman who had come to him from Michigan to Georgia for a job interview. She had become hysterical in his office, screaming words he could not comprehend. He called our psychologist friend Jim, who was able to calm her down. She left for her hotel with Jim's phone number.

In the middle of the night, Jim woke us with a problem. "Your friend is out of control again and the hotel wants her to leave. Not knowing what to do, Rog and Jim met at the hotel and finally decided to bring her to our house. Rog asked if she would like to come meet his wife. She seemed to feel it would help to talk to a woman- I do not know why. God knows. He brought her home. He introduced her and went to bed!

We had a peaceful visit about nothing important. I invited her to stay overnight, but as we prepared for bed, she again lost contact with reality, screaming in terror about things she seemed to be seeing. Leading her to the couch, I prayed for her to have peace. She quietly curled up with my blanket like a baby and closed her eyes, grabbing my hand tightly as though she feared floating away. Sitting on the floor next to her, I held her hand praying silently for answers. As long as I was with her, she slept. I dozed off and on during the night with her hand still in mine.

She woke up before dawn, shocking me from sleep with, "I have to get saved!"

I was shocked; I had not mentioned God at all to her. She prayed after me, repenting, (asking God to forgive her) and invited Jesus to take over her life.

What a transformation there was in her! We had a wonderful day together, studying the Bible and sharing our life experiences- except one big secret.

We went to bed that night, and all fell asleep exhausted. At 2AM I sat up in bed hearing Janet screaming into my bedroom, "I am leaving! There are Bibles in this house!"

Down the stairs she flew, and out the front door into the night. My knees knocked together so badly, I could hardly pull my slacks on! She was out of her mind, and had no idea where she was.

In the yard I realized an evil spirit causing great agitation was attacking her, and it was not submitting to me. I told her she now had to use her new authority to resist him. She began screaming at him, "Satan, I belong to Jesus. I am giving you "the books", your ring, and your cape! She threw something from her finger, but I never found a ring. She had been a Satanist. Her Christian grandfather was praying for her deliverance, and he got his answer. Janet has been doing very well ever since, once she learned what she had inherited from God. Everything!

□ □ □

A couple befriended my husband and me when we were younger. One day, Mary, a devout Catholic, called me. She was very frightened, and asked me to come quickly. I drove over, and her husband Gene opened the door and calmly invited me in. The room was cold as ice on this hot day, and I knew there was a presence that was not human! He asked me if I believed the devil is real, and then, in a very different voice than his, he said, "You are talking to him right now!" and told me he was the devil.

Gene had spent the afternoon chopping up all his furniture and shredding his wife's fur coat and clothing into small pieces. He had destroyed his entire house of its contents with his bare hands!

I prayed for Jesus to help me, grabbed Mary's hand and literally dragged her out, asking God to keep us from being stopped. I believe only prayer and the name of Jesus got us out without injury.

Mary stayed with us for a week, and went to a counselor. But she returned to him in a week! He either threatened her or found some way to keep her from leaving. Several people tried to talk to her, but she would not allow anyone to help her. She is still locked in a prison of fear twenty years later. I still pray for their freedom.

What is Cessationism?

The first time I heard the message of God's grace, His undeserved favor, I left that church, believing it was a false church! It is so foreign to many denominations that have been taught the concept of "cessationism." It is such a false belief, but somehow in these last days it has caught on in most churches. God warned this would happen in the end times and it is.

What the enemy means for evil, God turns
out for good. Romans 8:28

We are in the end times, meaning Christ is
about to return to earth and bring His
followers home to heaven. He promised it to
His disciples and it is still forthcoming. The
prophetic signs of His return have nearly all
come to pass. We will go into that later.

Jesus said in the end times there will be
great deception, to the extent that if it were
possible, even His chosen people would be
deceived. Jesus even said, "Will I find faith
on the earth when I return?" Satan goes to
the top, to those who influence others, in
order to deceive. He goes to the teachers.

"Cessationist" Christianity holds to the view
that the supernatural gifts such as healing,
speaking in tongues and prophesying were
used as signs to confirm the validity of who
Jesus and his followers were and that they
are no longer necessary for the church.
Some also believe the position of Apostle no
longer exists. Ask google the meaning of

cessationism. Ask your pastor what he believes as well. It is important.

One type of church teaches the Bible rather literally. Others leave out important information about the Holy Spirit, the third part of the Trinity. It begins in the seminaries where the future pastors are being taught what to preach. It is important to know to get through this life victoriously. We need all the tools God offers.

Satan's deception to divide the church with disagreements often involves the Holy Spirit. He plants lies in our minds. One lie is that God no longer baptizes or immerses us with His Spirit. He twists the verse that says: "When the perfect comes, tongues will pass away and knowledge will pass away." Some seminaries interpret that to mean "the perfect" is the completed New Testament. "Once it was completed, there was no longer any use for other tongues, so they are no longer available." It makes no sense. Knowledge has not yet passed away. As a matter of fact, God said in the end, knowledge would increase. We have not seen so much knowledge since the world began!

Some Christians view the miracles in the Bible as being limited to that time period when God was most forceful in proving his influence. In the Full Gospel circles, those that believe the Bible more literally, these miracles still occur and include healing and speaking in tongues.

This gift, the 'least of the spiritual gifts', but still important, is a private unknown language I assume Satan cannot understand, though there are times we speak in a known language, but there are two types of tongues. One is personal. I Cor.14:2 It is a miracle to be able to open your mouth and decide not to speak English and a real language comes out. Scientists have proved your frontal lobe is dormant while speaking this other language! It comes from the spirit.

It is not even logical to deny this gift exists today. There are over 200 million

Pentecostal Christians in the world. The most powerful ministries are those that simply accept the Bible as factual for today as well as in the days of the apostles and prophets of old.

So what do they believe, teach and manifest? They believe the book of Acts is for today. When Jesus left the earth, He said, "Go and tarry in Jerusalem, and wait for the Holy Spirit. He cannot come until I get to heaven. I will send Him to you." So 500 people who watched Jesus leave the earth in a cloud returned and waited in an upstairs hall or large room. They got a bit disillusioned, though, when it did not happen for ten more days, until the day of Pentecost, when people from all over the area were in the city to celebrate the feast.

By then, only 120 had stuck it out and remained. Suddenly the room was filled with a powerful wind-inside! Tongues of fire appeared on every head! And each one began babbling in strange languages! The spirit led them outside where foreigners heard them all speaking in their various languages, the message about Jesus! This is how the church spread around the world.

When the entire experience of this supernatural baptism is eliminated, all the gifts God has for us go in the trash as well, because it is this experience that brings in these wonderful gifts. You see miracles very rarely in those churches that do not teach that this is for today. You hardly ever hear about healings, and prophecy is not even allowed in these churches. They have also been taught that prophecy is simply preaching. It is so much more.

There are nine spiritual gifts that we can receive from the Holy Spirit. They vary with each person as God chooses to give different ones to each of us. There are gifts of healings, a gift of miracles, a gift of speaking in diverse tongues, a gift of interpreting the tongues, a gift of prophecy, a gift of supernatural knowledge, a gift of supernatural wisdom, a gift of discerning spirits, and a gift of special faith.

The dove is a symbol of the Holy Spirit. Doves have nine feathers on each side. One side symbolizes the nine gifts of the spirit. The other side signifies the nine fruits of the spirit. He has five tail feathers that stand for the fivefold leader ministry gifts: prophets, pastors, teachers, evangelists and apostles. Doves are interesting and unique. They mate for life, and tears come out of their eyes!

If you need a miracle from God, you need great faith. You need the power of the Holy Spirit to have great faith. You need to ask Jesus to baptize you (immerse you) with His Holy Spirit. Then you need to yield to Him and allow Him to come into you. If you ask, Jesus won't give you a stone or a scorpion, He said He will give you the Holy Spirit. He is already with you, and He will fill you with Himself. Then you will begin to see supernatural things happen. Healing and miracles are available to you in a deeper measure. Your ability to understand the Bible will become deeper, greater. A whole new dimension opens up, as you will see.

Yield your tongue but use your vocal cords and try to just let God use your voice. If you only get one word, speak it, and more words will gradually manifest. That is faith working.

You will desire meaty spiritual teaching, and not just milk, like babies drink. "Full gospel churches" and charismatic (means grace) churches will fulfill you in a way you may have never tasted. I hope this letter has enlightened and encouraged you! The best is yet to come!

He is "the same yesterday and today and forever" (Hebrews 13:8) and with that faith that God acts in the world today the same way as in ancient times.

The Second Blessing

Salvation is normally viewed as a long-term one-step process for Christians. In the Full Gospel Church, another level of salvation is recognized. It is called the 'second blessing' and those baptized in the Full Gospel Church make it their foremost goal.

The first blessing is secured through believing Jesus was crucified, dead, and resurrected and confessing it. Then being baptized in water is the outward sign of our belief. Reaching the second blessing is simply asking Jesus to baptize us with His Holy Spirit and trusting Him.

Spiritual healing arises from the belief in miracles. Prayer is considered an essential step in overcoming disease. Energetic services where people seemingly recover from disability or sickness immediately are flagships of Full Gospel and Pentecostal services.

There has been controversy as some churches encourage people to bypass modern medical intervention and rely solely on faith healing and prayer. It should be emphasized, though, that is not the usual belief of most Full Gospel churches. Most believe God uses doctors and knowledge as well as faith in healing.

Faith goes beyond rituals and dogma, and extends into action and full involvement in religious services. Being expressive during church is a large part of Pentecostal practices.

Signs of a Need for Deliverance

Yes, Christians can be oppressed with a demon, but not in their spirit. The body or mind can be influenced, but there is a solution. Not to worry. Help is on the way! The presence of a demon is often detected as a person with a discernment gift recognizes it. I Corinthians 12:10. Hebrews 5:14 suggests that mature Christians have their senses exercised to discern good and evil.

Symptoms are psychological and physical. Emotional signs are those that dominate the person even contrary to his nature, like fear, tension, jealousy and so forth. Another sign is moods, ranging from incessant talking to depression. Look for forms of religious error or bondage, such as submission to unbiblical prohibitions or doctrines, severe self-discipline, refusal to eat normal diets, superstitions and all idolatry (materialism, living to eat and drink, appetite first, pleasures, titles, wealth, sports and so forth.) Resorting to using charms, psychics and the like, enslaving habits, blasphemy or unclean language, and violent or persistent opposition to the truth of scripture. This is a partial list but sufficient.

Physical signs of a need for deliverance

A few out of many are chronic illnesses, altered state of consciousness, difficulty in receiving the baptism in the Holy Spirit, hearing voices, imaginary playmates as a child, compulsions

What are the conditions for deliverance?

1. A correct diagnosis. I Corinthians 9:26.
2. A believer to minister deliverance with authority in Jesus 'name. Luke 10:17; Acts 16:18
   A. Must have Holy Spirit's power. Matthew 12:28.
   B. Must have the anointing of the Spirit to set the captive at liberty when they have been bruised. Luke 4:18
   C. The one ministering must understand the principles defining

conditions for: forgiveness of sins, legal basis of redemption through Christ's blood.

3. Spending time privately counseling about past events.
4. The minister must have humility toward God and others.

Client preparation

1. Humility-to resist the devil. James 4-7.
2. Honesty. Psalm, 32:1-6.
3. Confession of sins. I John 1:9; James 5:16.
4. Willingness to forsake the acts and desires.
5. Forgiveness of others and self-most common barrier. Hebrews 12:15.

The Lord's Prayer covers it. Claim the promise in Joel 2:32.

Now for Housecleaning

Demons have a legal right to enter a home if bad things happened in that home. Imagine a house of prostitution, or a place where someone committed suicide, or even a home where a person died who had spirits in him. Where are they going to go? The Bible says they seek a place to reside, and if the house is swept clean that they left, they can return with seven more wicked than they were, unless that person continues to walk with God.   Luke 11:24-26. How can this be prevented?

Examine your house. Ask the Lord if there is anything in it that gives the spirits the right to remain there. Pray over your pets and take dominion over any spirit that might have headed for them when it left you. (Remember the pigs?) Pray over your home and anoint it with oil. Many people touch the doors and windows with a drop of oil as a symbol of the Holy Spirit's protection.

If you are unaware of items that may give spirits permission to bother you, look it up on your phone. Google knows everything! Some examples are peace symbols, circles with an upside down cross inside, Indian dream catchers, Buddhas, Ouija boards, New age symbols, books, jewelry. The list is endless. Beware of certain TV programs. The eye gate must be protected, especially for our children. Dungeons and Dragons games can harm people that don't have a clue. Harry Potter books and movies. Our children are very susceptible and don't know what to do when attacked. The world is full of evil.

Don't give the objects to others. In the Bible the new Christians had a huge bonfire and burned all their occult books and things.

Prayer: Dear Father in heaven, forgive me for having these things in my possession. I renounce all involvements that are against your Word. I resist all evil spirits in the name of Jesus and I plead Jesus' blood over my family, myself, and all that we have.

Thank you for being made a curse for me so I can be free! Amen.

In case you wonder if this is scriptural, here is some evidence.

I Peter 5:8 Be alert and of sober mind. Your enemy the devil prowls about like a roaring lion looking for someone to devour. Resist him, standing firm in the faith…10 God will restore you after you have suffered a little while…

2 Corinthians 11:4 For if someone comes to you and preaches a Jesus other than the Jesus we preached, or if you *receive a different spirit* from the Spirit you received…you put up with it…14 …Satan masquerades as an angel of light.

Matthew 10:1 When He had called unto him his twelve disciples, He gave them power against unclean spirits, to cast them out, and to heal…

Mark 1:26, 27 Throwing him into convulsions, the unclean spirit cried out with a loud voice and came out of him. 27 They were all amazed, so that they debated among themselves, saying, "What is this? A new teaching with authority! He commands even the unclean spirits and they obey Him."

Revelation 12:9 And the great dragon was cast out, that old serpent, called the Devil and Satan, which deceives the whole world; he was cast out into the earth, and his angels were cast out with him.

2 Corinthians 4:3,4 ...gospel is veiled to those who are perishing, whose minds the god of this age has blinded, who do not believe...

I Timothy 4:1 The Spirit clearly says that in later times some will abandon the faith and follow deceiving spirits and things taught by demons.

2 Corinthians 12:7 ...I was given a thorn in my flesh, a messenger of Satan.

I John 4:4 You, dear children, are from God and have overcome them, because the one who is in you is greater than the one who is in the world.

God is our Deliverer.

He is the same today, yesterday and forever.

Ask anything in His name according to His will and it shall be done unto you.

Proverbs 11:21 (KJV) *Though* hand *join* in hand, the wicked shall not be unpunished: but **the seed of the righteous shall be delivered.**

Proverbs 11:8-9 (KJV) The righteous is delivered out of trouble, and the wicked cometh in his stead. [9] An hypocrite with *his* mouth destroyeth his neighbour: but through knowledge shall **the just be delivered.**

Psalm 22:5 (KJV) They cried unto thee, and were delivered: they trusted in thee, and were not confounded.

Psalm 33:16 (KJV) There is no king saved by the multitude of an host: a mighty man is not delivered by much strength

Psalm 34:4 (KJV) I sought the LORD, and he heard me, and delivered me from all my fears.

Psalm 54:7 (KJV) For he hath delivered me

out of all trouble: and mine eye hath seen *his desire* upon mine enemies.

Psalm 55:18 (KJV) He hath delivered my soul in peace from the battle *that was* against me: for there were many with me.

Psalm 56:13 (KJV) For thou hast delivered my soul from death: *wilt* not *thou deliver* my feet from falling, that I may walk before God in the light of the living?

Psalm 81:7 (KJV) Thou calledst in trouble, and I delivered thee; I answered thee in the secret place of thunder: I proved thee at the waters of Meribah. Selah.

Psalm 107:6 (KJV) Then they cried unto the LORD in their trouble, *and* he delivered them out of their distresses.

Psalm 107:20 (KJV) *He sent his word, and healed them, and delivered them from their destructions.*

Ezekiel 33:9 (KJV) Nevertheless, if thou warn the wicked of his way to turn from it; if he do not turn from his way, he shall die in his iniquity; but thou hast delivered thy soul.

Daniel 12:1 (KJV) And at that time shall Michael stand up, the great prince which standeth for the children of thy people: and there shall be a time of trouble, such as never was since there was a nation *even* to that same time: and at that time thy people shall be delivered, every one that shall be found written in the book.

Joel 2:32 (KJV) And it shall come to pass, *that* <u>**whosoever shall call on the name of the LORD shall be delivered:**</u> for in mount Zion and in Jerusalem shall be deliverance, as the LORD hath said, and in the remnant whom the LORD shall call.

Habakkuk 2:9 (KJV) Woe to him that coveteth an evil covetousness to his house, that he may set his nest on high, that he may be delivered from the power of evil!

Acts 7:10 (KJV) And delivered him out of all his afflictions, and gave him favour and wisdom in the sight of Pharaoh king of Egypt; and he made him governor over Egypt and all his house.

Romans 8:21 (KJV) Because the creature itself also shall be delivered from the bondage of corruption into the glorious liberty of the children of God.

Colossians 1:13 (KJV) Who hath **delivered us from the power of darkness,** and hath translated *us* into the kingdom of his dear Son:

2 Timothy 4:7 (KJV) I have fought a good fight, I have finished *my* course, I have kept the faith:

2 Timothy 3:11 (KJV) Persecutions, **afflictions,** which came unto me at Antioch, at Iconium, at Lystra; what persecutions I endured: but **out of *them* all the Lord delivered me.**

1 Thessalonians 1:10 (KJV) And to wait for his Son from heaven, whom he raised from the dead, *even* Jesus, which **delivered us from the wrath to come.**

Psalm 144:2 (KJV) My goodness, and my fortress; my high tower, and my deliverer; my shield, and *he* in whom I trust; who subdueth my people under me.

Psalm 70:5 (KJV) But I *am* poor and needy: make haste unto me, O God: thou *art* my help and my deliverer; O LORD, make no tarrying.

Psalm 18:2 (KJV) The LORD *is* my rock, and my fortress, and my deliverer; my God, my strength, in whom I will trust; my buckler, and the horn of my salvation, *and* my high tower.

When you have done all, stand firm and see the salvation of the Lord.

Wrath to come:

Matthew 3:7 (KJV) But when he saw many of the Pharisees and Sadducees come to his baptism, he said unto them, O generation of vipers, who hath warned you to flee from the wrath to come?

Romans 1:18 (KJV) For the wrath of God is revealed from heaven against all ungodliness and unrighteousness of men, who hold the truth in unrighteousness;

Romans 2:5 (KJV) But after thy hardness and impenitent heart treasurest up unto thyself wrath against the day of wrath and revelation of the righteous judgment of God;

Romans 5:9 (KJV) Much more then, being now justified by his blood, we shall be saved from wrath through him.

Colossians 3:6 (KJV) For which things' sake the wrath of God cometh on the children of disobedience:

1 Thessalonians 1:10 (KJV) And to wait for his Son from heaven, whom he raised from the dead, *even* Jesus, which delivered us   from   the   wrath   to   come.

1 Thessalonians 2:16 (KJV) Forbidding us to speak to the Gentiles that they might be saved, to fill up their sins alway: for the wrath is come upon them to the uttermost.

1 Thessalonians 5:9 (KJV) For God hath not appointed us to wrath, but to obtain salvation by our Lord Jesus Christ,

Revelation 6:16-17 (KJV) And said to the mountains and rocks, Fall on us, and hide us from the face of him that sitteth on the throne, and from the wrath of the Lamb: [17] For the great day of his wrath is come; and who   shall   be   able   to   stand?

Revelation 11:18 (KJV) And the nations were angry, and thy wrath is come, and the time of the dead, that they should be judged, and that thou shouldest give reward unto thy servants the prophets, and to the saints, and them that fear thy name, small and great; and shouldest destroy them which destroy the earth.

Luke 21:36 (KJV) Watch ye therefore, and pray always, that ye may be accounted worthy to escape all these things that shall come to pass, and to stand before the Son of man.

Hebrews 12:25 (KJV) See that ye refuse not him that speaketh. For if they escaped not who refused him that spake on earth, much more *shall not* we *escape*, if we turn away from him that *speaketh* from heaven:

Acts 14:22 (KJV) Confirming the souls of the disciples, *and* exhorting them to continue in the faith, and that we must through much tribulation enter into the kingdom of God.

Matthew 24:21 (KJV) For then shall be great tribulation, such as was not since the beginning of the world to this time, no, nor ever shall be.

Matthew 24:29 (KJV) Immediately after the tribulation of those days shall the sun be darkened, and the moon shall not give her light, and the stars shall fall from heaven, and the powers of the heavens shall be shaken:

Epilogue

I would love to hear your remarks, good or bad. All of them are valid. My Email is granparrott@gmail.com. I would enjoy your experiences, too. I love to read.

Other books I have written can be found on Amazon and Kindle. You will find several subjects there, addiction recoveries, amazing moments in our lives, dreams and visions, plus many more. All teaching is backed up with scriptures. Check it out. God bless you!

Judy Parrott

A Life Worth Living (my autobiography)
Alien and other Mysteries.
A Time to Heal
Break Every Chain (How to overcome addictions)
Dreams and Visions of the Future.
Evidence of His Presence.(Addictions)
Heart to Heart (like Jesus Calling)
*His Journey to Eternity (*my husband Rog's life story)
Motorcycle Miracles and other Stories
Mysterious Wonders.
Quicksand-about addictions.
Shout from the Housetops (like Jesus Calling)
Supernatural Events from God.

27655736R00100

Made in the USA
Columbia, SC
04 October 2018